In My Despair

Printed in the United States of America

First Printing, 2019

ISBN 978-0-9994726-4-4

Happie Face Publishing Company
www.hfpublishingco.com

de·spair
/dəˈspɛr/

Noun

- The complete loss or absence of hope.

  Synonyms: hopelessness, disheartened, discouragement, anguish, unhappiness.

  Verb

- *Lose or be without hope*

Dedication

This book is lovingly dedicated to my personal superhero - my wonderful grandmother for her undying love and support. Your sacrifices will never be forgotten.

To my husband and children who have shown me patience as I wrote this book: A lot of my days were darkened but your support carried me through.

Thank you.

All names in the text have been changed to protect the identities of the innocent and the not so innocent with the exception of the following: Monique Fisher & Jac'Queena James.

TABLE OF CONTENTS

PROLOGUE

When you're asked to play a game, what do you expect? Fun, excitement, and lots of laughter – given that you actually know how to play, right? But what happens when you're forced to play a game that has no instructions?

I was such a young girl when life dealt me a hand that I was not yet ready to play. Shucks, I didn't even know the rules yet – not that there were any - but I knew I hated playing. Unfortunately for me, I was going to be forced to play along until I was grown.

CHAPTER ONE

I was born in the city of Chester, PA in August of 1975. My mother and my father were not together. My father was around, but he wasn't really a big part of my life. I saw him every now and then - just enough for me to know who he was, I guess. My mom and I lived in Upland with my grandmother, my two aunts, my little cousin, his father and my uncle and boy was life sweet! We had a four-bedroom house with a nice, big back yard with just enough space for me to run around. Even though I had to share a room with my mom and my aunt, it was as if the room was all mine because all my stuffed animals, toys, and drawings consumed the space. Sure it was loud, there were fights, and I got into some trouble, but I felt loved and that's what was most important.

Anyway, I was my mother's first child and the first grandchild too, so needless to say, I was spoiled but not rotten... well okay, maybe I was a *little* rotten.

Overall, I was a good kid, but I was *far* from an angel though.

I got up to my own mischief and little white lies were my forte, though my grandmother would argue *"there is no color to a lie, a lie is just a lie"*. I had gotten pretty good at lying, but I didn't always get away with them. I once decided that I was going to get a jerry curl because everyone on my block had one - it was the eighties, don't laugh. I told my aunt Stacy, who is a beautician, that my dad said that he would pay her to give me one. She agreed and I got a curl, but my dad wasn't going to be paying a penny because he didn't actually know anything about it. My mom was so mad at me that she threatened not take care of my hair, and I'll tell you one thing – she made good on that threat. I was six years old and didn't know anything about taking care of my own hair, so consequently my hair fell out and my hair texture changed. My family was so mad at me for lying about that, but hey, I was only a kid. Of course, that incident didn't stop me from lying, but it was one lie that I really wish that I hadn't told.

I loved living with my grandmother because she was always bringing something home for me, her "Pippi" - that's what she used to call me. No matter how my grandmother felt on any particular day, she didn't mind if I climbed on her lap so she could hold and rock me in her arms. She made sure that everyone was nice to me including my uncle who would pick on me all the time. My grandmother was my everything. Then there was our dog, Sheba. Sheba was a tan and white Germen Shepard and everywhere that I went, Sheba was sure to go. She would even follow me to school, and despite it being against the rules, I loved having my four-legged friend follow me around. Sheba was my best friend.

We had a full house, and everyone was into their own thing, but I still managed to be the center of attention. So, imagine my surprise when my mother announced to everyone that she was getting married. I was *not* happy. She had been dating Jason for a while, but marriage? No way! Sure, mom was a couple months pregnant, but that still was't a good enough excuse to get married. Shoot, she wasn't married to my dad when she gave birth to me, so what difference would it make if she didn't marry Jason? At first, I didn't like Jason because I thought he was going to steal my thunder, but as time went on, there was something about him that really was not right. Even Sheba didn't like him.

I will never forget the Spring of 1982, because that's when

my mother tied the knot. I cried like a baby during the service but I remember looking around and noticing that I was not the only one upset about this ridiculous occasion. Everyone knows that the birth of a child, graduation, and one's wedding day are supposed to be the most joyful events in life, so what was going on? Instead of happiness filling the warm air, there was nothing but sorrow – it was as if it was a funeral.

"Is there anyone here that objects to these two people being united in holy matrimony? Let them speak now or forever hold their peace." The preacher questioned the crowd. He must have sensed that I was not happy about this ceremony and was giving me a chance to say so, but I couldn't bring myself to be the bearer of drama. I quickly looked around hoping that someone – *anyone* – would speak up and say something. No one said a single word. Gosh, why did they let such a perfect opportunity pass by? If I didn't think my mom would have killed me, I would have jumped up and shouted, "She can't marry him because he's crazy!" But, I had better sense than that. I was young, but I was no fool.

"Ladies and gentlemen, I now pronounce to you Mr. and Mrs. Jason James," the preacher announced. I could have fainted. It was a beautiful day and the sun shined as we stood in the back yard, but all I could feel was a dark cloud hanging over my head. A few days after the wedding, my mom and I found ourselves at Philadelphia International Airport hopping on a plane to Mississippi, our new home. I hated that we were moving away, but we had to since Jason was stationed there.

"This is going to be a new start for us," my mom stated. The thing was, I didn't want a new start; I was happy with how things were. But it made no difference; I still was being forced on that plane.

It was my first time on an airplane, and honestly, I was scared, but I enjoyed every minute of the ride with the exception of my ears getting clogged. *So, maybe moving would turn out just the same; maybe things would work out* I thought. My mom gave me a wad of gum to chew to prevent my ears from blocking and it really worked, but boy were my jaws sore.

When we arrived in Mississippi, Jason was waiting and he actually appeared to be happy to see us, but I was not happy to see him. We had to walk awfully far to get to the car, so I was happy when I finally got a chance to rest those dogs. Thank goodness we were headed straight to our new house because a feeling I had never felt came over me. I could feel my stomach turning and my mouth getting warmer.

"I feel sick," I murmured. Mom quickly cut her eyes back at me. I looked up at her, with eyes that asked for help, but she remained silent.

"You better not throw up in my car," Jason growled. It was bad enough that I felt horrible, but his attitude towards me made me feel even worse. I kept quiet and covered my mouth for the rest of the ride.

In about 30 minutes, we pulled up to our new abode. It was a cute one-bedroom house that reminded me of the large, empty doll house. As soon as I walked in, I marveled at all the space. There was only one wall that separated the downstairs and there was no real layout to the floor plan aside from the furniture placement. I walked up the wooden stairs and I was shocked to learn that there was no real room. There was only a large space, much like a studio, and the only things up there were my new bunk bed and Jason and my mom's queen-sized bed. Now, I was used to sharing rooms, but was I really going to have to share with *this* guy?

We were far from living a fairytale life, but my mother still appeared to be happy. We didn't get to get out and do much. Money must have been tight because going out for ice cream was the highlight of the month. I was also very lonely; all of my family was far away and I missed them so much. I couldn't visit or sleep over on weekends - I couldn't even pick up the phone and call them. Sure, I had made friends at my new school, but it wasn't the same. There was only one thing that kept me from screaming, and that was the fact that my mom was going to have a baby soon.

One night, my mom was cooking pork chops, rice, and veggies while I was in the living area playing with my dolls and Jason was at the dining room table going through some paperwork. Suddenly, we heard what appeared to be a pot dropping, so Jason jolted up and I followed. When we went into the kitchen area, I could see peas scattering on the floor. Jason's high yellow face was now red, my mom had tears streaming down her face, and I guess shocked washed across mine. Instinctively, I attempted to help my mom clean up the mess by gathering up the scurrying peas, when Jason became a scarier version of himself. He became the person I was afraid he would be.

He screamed, "Mind your mother f**king business and get the hell out!"

I bolted out of the kitchen so fast and got half way up the stairs before I realized that I left my doll, so I snuck back downs to get it. Just as I scooped my doll up, Jason yanked my arm.

"You're one hard-headed son of a bi**h"!" he griped as he shoved me with his humungous hands.

"I'm- I'm going upstairs!" I trembled as I backed away, eventually taking off running again. When I made it to our room, I sat on my bed, shut my eyes tight, and rocked back and forth. *What did I do wrong?* I thought to myself. *I was only checking on my mom and I got out of the kitchen when he told me to.* He never said for me to go upstairs so it didn't make sense that he screamed at me again when he saw me in the living room.

After that night, I started to hear more and more arguments break out. Him fighting my mom became the norm. Sometimes it seemed like I fell asleep with them fighting and I woke up to them going at it again. Days eventually started running together and I stopped being able to keep track.

One morning, my mom woke me up late for school, so she rushed me all morning, even through breakfast. I was already annoyed, but then Jason came in the kitchen and asked, "Is this my eggs?" pointing to his plate and added to my irritation level. I did everything in my power to pay him no mind. I really wished he could just disappear, but since that wasn't going to happen, pretending like he wasn't there was the next best thing.

"Yes, they're yours," Mom nodded. The next thing I knew, he grabbed some eggs from the fridge and cracked them over her head.

"This is not how I like my eggs!" he shouted. I watched wide-eyed and disturbed as my mom stood still in complete shock. She did nothing, while he stomped away. At that moment, I was convinced that the man that I thought was only crazy for taking away my attention was truly crazy fo' real! It seemed like nothing was ever good enough for him, so he made it a point to express it whenever he wanted.

That October, I was dragged to the hospital in the middle of the night because my mom was in labor; somehow I was tired and ecstatic all at the same time. After waiting for what seemed like an eternity, the doctor announced the arrival of my new sibling.

"It's a girl! You're a big sister now," the doctor said to me.

"What's my sister's name?"

"Jac'Queena," Jason proudly stated.

What! Jac who? I thought to myself.

"It means 'Jason's girl'", he explained. *Jason's girl? Whatever!* I couldn't wait to see my little sister, though. I just wanted to play with her, but to my disappointment, I was only able to look at her through a window. I looked around confused and worried because I thought they showed me the wrong baby; she was so pale and funny looking, but I still managed to fall in love with her. She was peaceful and without a care in the world. I stared at her, wishing I could learn her secret.

"Monique, it's time to go home," Jason grumbled.

Already?! I thought. I didn't even get a chance to hold my sister. I sauntered towards him, but not before taking one last look at my Jac'Queena. As we walked out, I turned around hoping to see my mother and sister coming behind us, but all I saw was an empty hallway. At that very moment, a weird feeling came over me.

"Where is mommy?" I inquired.

He replied in a stern voice, "She has to stay here for a couple of days and then she'll be home." *What?! In a couple of days?*

15

Panic washed throughout my body, but I tried to keep myself calm. I really didn't want to be left alone with Jason because there was no telling how he would treat me. I mean, it wasn't like he ever hit me or anything — I wasn't even sure if he ever hit my mom or not, but what I did know is that he had a temper and that he could yell so loud, a deaf man could hear him.

It was just about the break of day when we arrived home. I was so tired and just wanted to go to bed. I climbed into the top bunk and snuggled under the covers, but as soon as I dozed off, Jason started moving furniture around. I groggily rose from my slumber and watched him reorganize the room we all shared, presumably to make room for the baby.

He was in his own world that day, and I really do believe he forgot about me. Consequently, I was alone and bored all day, so to pass the time, I colored. I loved to color. I didn't have anyone else around my age, so coloring gave me a way to create the perfect friends to keep me company when I was lonely.

When it was time for bed, Jason found me and tossed a nightgown on my bed. I simply stared at it.

"That doesn't fit me anymore," I calmly explained to him. In his typical fashion, he roared back at me.

16

"Put the d*mn thing on and go to bed!"

I turned my back to him and forced the nightgown on. Just like I said, it didn't fit me at all and was short enough that you could see my butt.

As I climbed up the ladder to the top bunk, I heard his voice say, "Girls shouldn't sleep in their underwear. Take them off."

"But I always sleep with them on," I replied.

"Take them off, you'll sleep better," he said again, and this time, he was demanding. I reluctantly pulled them off and laid them next to me. I had no idea what was going on - I was so terrified and all I wanted to do was to go to sleep. I shut my eyes real tight and said my prayers hoping they would shield me from danger.

"Now I lay me down to sleep, I pray the lord my soul to keep. And if I die before I wake, I pray the lord my soul He'll take. Lord please bring my mom and new baby sister home soon. Amen".

I was way too uneasy to drift off to sleep immediately, but eventually, I did doze off. I didn't know what time it was, but I knew that it was in the middle of the night. Thinking I was dreaming, I felt something touch my leg, so I moved over. I felt it again, so this time I opened my eyes and when I looked, I saw Jason's hand creep up the side of my bed that was against the wall like a curious spider. I froze like a popsicle as his fingers slowly made their way to my vagina. When I tried to turn away, he firmly grabbed my leg and without a word, I knew he was telling me to stay still so that he could do what he wanted to me.

I was only seven years old; I had no clue what he was doing, but I knew it was wrong. All I could do was cry and cry some more as I silently prayed that he would stop. At that moment, I no longer just disliked him – I *hated* him. When he finished, he left me only with racing thoughts. I held on to my blanket tight and curled into a little ball with my back facing the wall. I couldn't bring myself to move, let alone get up – I was too afraid of what would happen to me.

I stared at the wall for the rest of the night and into the morning. I desperately wanted to fade away, but I couldn't because of the terror I felt. Only one thought filled my headspace: *why?* Then I thought only about how I could avoid Jason until my mom got home, but it was hard considering there was no place to hide away.

Thankfully, I didn't have to spend another night with Jason alone because my mom and sister came home the next morning. My mind and emotions were all over the place; I wanted to tell my mother what happened, but was afraid. Yet and still, I had so much excitement bubbling up inside of me that I could have burst. I was finally going to have someone to play with. My mom was exhausted, so she didn't mind if I played mommy for a few hours, but Jason did. I was "too young" to hold the baby, "too young" to feed the baby, and "too young" to change the baby's diaper, too young to blah blah blah. Jason made sure I didn't get to spend time with Jac'Queena – 'Queena for short – but that was fine – the baby thing was not all that fun anyway; all she did was sleep and when she was awake she cried like a wounded kitten.

Despite all of the restrictions that Jason put on me in regards to his daughter, I still wanted to be with my little sister as much as I could. Every day after school, I would rush home just to see her tiny fingers and toes. I don't know why, but I counted them all the time; maybe I thought they could fall off or something. She was so small and so fragile, I did think at times that it was possible for me to break her.

The holiday season came quickly and Christmas was rapidly approaching. There was only a week or two left until Christmas and we still didn't have a Christmas tree yet. Maybe we just couldn't afford one, but this was my first Christmas without a tree to decorate and it was a bit depressing. Decorating the Christmas tree was one of my favorite things to do – I looked forward to it, almost as much as opening gifts. A few days passed, and still no tree, so I asked my mom if we were going to have anything to decorate for Christmas. She took a minute before answering.

"Sure we will. Come on get your coat on," she smiled at me. I jumped up and ran to the closet to get my coat as I hummed, *"we are going to get a tree, going to get a tree, going to get a tree-ee just for me."*

"Ready mom!" I shouted with excitement and the biggest smile on my face. My mom came out the kitchen with a couple of empty grocery bags and hooked them to the handles of my sisters' stroller, but I didn't think anything of it.

"Come on let's go!" I insisted. I skipped outside as I continued to hum *"we are going to get a tree, going to get a tree, going to get a tree-ee just for me."* I didn't even get to feel the crisp winter air on my cheeks before I was interrupted.

"Monique!" mom called out to me.

"Huh?" I answered.

"Pick out some pine cones and put them in this bag," she said. I stared at her for a moment, confused, but shrugged it off – after all, we were out of the house and were finally going to get a tree! I hopped, skipped, and jumped around the yard, gathering as many pine cones as possible. Big ones, small ones, skinny ones, fat ones – I collected them all and dropped them in the plastic bag. All the while, I could see mom watching me, smiling as I danced across the yard with holiday cheer.

I scrounged the area for all that I could find and when the bag was full, we headed back toward the house. I thought she must have forgotten her money or something because we hadn't even gotten our tree yet. We went into the house and when my mom said, "don't take your coat off", I let out a sigh of relief. Surely we were about to head back out to Christmas tree lot or find something around here.

"Okay, come on," she said as she opened up the back door with a can of gold spray paint in one hand and the bag of pine cones in her other hand.

"Help me line up the pine cones in a row." I was still clueless as to what we were doing, but I did what she asked. We carefully placed the cones in a line on the ground and when we finished, mom grabbed the can of spray paint.

"Watch out now," she said holding me back as she began to spray the miniature trees.

"Mom! When are we going to go and get the tree?" I yanked on her coat sleeve.

"We're not going to get a tree", she said. Before I could ask why, she blurted out, "you'll see." About fifteen minutes after they dried, mom gathered all the cones and headed back inside. I watched her as she nicely placed them in a circle on the floor. She presented the display to me as if it was supposed to be just as good of an alternative, and though it wasn't a tree, I must say it was nice.

I learned a little later why there wasn't a tree. Jason was a Jehovah Witness and since they don't celebrate holidays that meant I wasn't going to be getting my tree or gifts. It was a sad Christmas.

Several weeks passed and business went on as usual. Jason

went to work and mom stayed home with Jac'Queena while I went to school. One day, Jason came home from work and caught me playing with my sister and snapped. Jason and my mom began arguing, to which then I saw him get in my mother's face as if he wanted to smack the taste out of her mouth. I couldn't tell you what he said because it was all a raging blur. Later that night he threw us all out in the snow. We had nowhere to go, so my mom walked me and my sister to a nearby convenience store. We walked around that store so long that my little feet began to hurt, but mom needed to clear her head and figure out what we were going to do.

After weighing her options and realizing that her husband was not coming for us, she called my grandmother collect. My grandmother told her to call the police, which she did, and the police made sure we were able to get back in the house to get some of our belongings.

"Can you take me to my family?" I whispered to an officer, but he ignored me. We packed up what we could carry and the police took us to a nearby shelter to stay. I didn't want to stay there because we had to sleep in a room filled with tons of other people, but it was better than going back to the house – that was the *last* place I wanted to be. Well, I guess what I wanted didn't matter much because we were home the next day.

Months had gone by since he touched me, so I figured I'd be okay in that respect, but I let my guard down too early. Since he was mad at my mother for calling the cops, he slept in the bottom bunk. I was sound asleep, when all of a sudden, my eyes shot open. He was hovering over me, and while one hand was over my mouth, his other hand motioned for me to keep quiet.

"Sshhhh," he hissed. It sent shivers down my spine and I froze up again as he leaned over me.

"I am going to touch you here," he said pointing to the same place he touched me before. "and you better not say a word. If you do, I'll kill you". Terrified of the repercussions, I nodded my head without a word and closed my eyes tight as he took advantage of me once more. For a second, I thought to scream. Mom was right there – she would have heard and she definitely would have helped me, but I couldn't risk it; if there was one thing I knew about Jason, it was that he didn't make threats – he made promises. From that night on, whenever he and my mother would fight, I got a visit from him.

For some reason we moved to Alabama; I believe Jason was

transferred there, however, we didn't live there long. We moved to Savannah, GA almost a year or so later to live with his father. I had hoped that things would get better for me – and it seemed like they did. After all, we were in a bigger house, I started a new school, I made new friends, and things calmed down with Jason and my mom. Maybe 'Queena was the reason for all the peace and joy.

I for one was happy for the move. I loved going to my new school, Butler Elementary. It was in a really nice neighborhood and was filled with people of all colors. Sitting on the bus watching the river, trees, and the sky pass me by for those fifteen minutes brought me some serenity. One day while on my way to school and in my own little world, I saw an alligator peak it's head out of the water and man that was awesome. Every day when the school bus would drive past the river, I would look for the alligator as if I were looking for a friend.

At that time, I was eight years old, in the second grade, and was doing exceptionally well in school. I got good grades and I even started to get involved with sports and other school activities. My life, for once, was normal again. I was like any other child. I would come home from school, do my homework, and then go outside to play until the street lights came on. I found out that my grandmother's brother played the guitar for the song, "Bustin' Loose" by Chuck Brown and the Soul Searchers, which I bragged about often. It seemed like every time that song came on I would be outside and my friends and I would dance as if it was our theme song or something.

Finally, the end of the school year came, and I was promoted to the third grade. I was excited about continuing my schooling there, I had just celebrated my ninth birthday, and 'Queena was running around like a little Flow Jo. Life truly was good again.

One day, shortly before school started back up, Jason came home from work very upset. My mother knew that he was steaming and I guess she didn't want any drama, so she left the house to pick up my sister, leaving him and I home alone. I continued to color and to pay him no mind, but after slamming doors and grabbing a cold drink, he turned his attention to me.

"Go put on your old gym shorts," he told me. His eyes were crazed.

Panicked, I attempted to stall my way out of his demand. "I-i-i-i-i - Um, I don't know where they are," I stuttered as I began collecting my crayons. I knew exactly where they were. My mom put them in a bag to take to the Salvation Army because they were too small.

"You have two minutes to find them," he said in a cold, dead voice as he sat down on the couch and took off his boots. With my stomach in knots, I left the living room to go and put on the shorts. It didn't take long for me find them, but I couldn't bring myself to put them on. I held them in my hands for as long as I could, hoping mom would turn up with 'Queena just in the nick of time.

"Monique! Come on! What the hell you doing?" Jason called to me. I sighed deeply and slipped the shorts on. When I came back, I immediately noticed a navy blue towel laid out on the floor.

"Turn around. Bend over," Jason grunted. "Come here and lay down."

"Why?" I asked shaking. He glared at me with stoked fires in his dark eyes.

"Are you questioning me? Lay down!"
His voice alone made my whole body quake; I was shaking like a leaf on a tree, but I reluctantly followed his command. As I laid on the floor, he unzipped his pants and pulled out his

manhood. He then kneeled down and began to rub my upper thigh with it. Disgusted and afraid, I thought, *What the heck is he doing!*

"Open your legs" he growled. I held my legs together as tight as I could before he pried them apart. He began rubbing my private area with his penis and my legs couldn't help but shake vigorously. All I could do was whimper and despite all the tears that flowed out of my eyes, he continued to violate me. He told me to lift up and he pulled my gym shorts off along with my underwear and proceeded to rub my bare skin as he panted. Suddenly, I felt his penis on my vagina and before I could brace myself, he attempted to jam himself into me. When that didn't work, he grabbed some Vaseline, put a glob of it on me, and shoved his tool into me. It was like trying to fit a camel in the eye of the needle – it just wouldn't fit unless you forced it.

I screamed, "Ouch! It hurts! Stop it, please, stop it!" He continued to go in and out of me as I pleaded for mercy. He didn't stop and he didn't care. I felt his hot breath hit my face with every pant and I couldn't escape it. The more I screamed, the more I felt trapped and worn out. I was in a closing cocoon and I was desperate to get out. The only thing I wanted in that moment was to hear the front door open and for my mom to save me. Time slowed down so quickly and I felt like it was never going to end.

"Go clean yourself up," he finally said to me. As much as I wanted to jump up and run out of there, I just laid there on the floor in pain and in a stupor.

"I said go clean-up! And when your mom comes home, you better not tell her anything or I'll kill you, do you hear me? I'll kill all of y'all!" He emphasized the word *kill*, and I knew he meant it.

I gradually rose, but could barely move my legs. I shuffled into the bathroom like a newborn doe, locked the door, and turned on the water. Tears seamlessly flowed nonstop. I grabbed my washcloth to wipe myself off and barely looked down for a second when I noticed blood on my thighs. I examined the crimson streams and when I wiped myself, I realized they were coming from me. I began to shake again and became lightheaded, so I curled up on the floor and closed my eyes. I took about 20 minutes to recoup as I wondered if I was in a bad dream. Peace had no place near me in that moment and I understood that when I heard pounding at the door. It wasn't a

29

dream after all.

"Get yourself together and get out of there," Jason barked. I waited for him to leave before I crept out the bathroom to get my clothes. I slid them on as fast as I could, given the fact that I felt broken inside and out and eased myself to the front door. I was hoping to see my mom walking down the street with 'Queena, but all I saw was the sun shining, the leaves rustling in the light summer breeze, and all sense of hope fading away. I could have used a lot of things at that moment, but what I wanted most was to get away.

I stepped out on the front porch, still shaken up but embraced the clean, brisk air that fell upon my face – it certainly beat having to inhale the sour stench of Jason and his iniquities. I slowly sat down on the porch step, hoping that if I just wished hard enough, my grandmom would appear right in front of me, but I was going to have to settle for my mom. Mom made her way up the street with my sister and a bag in her hand, completely oblivious. Normally, if I were outside playing and I saw them walking, I would run up to them with cheerful smile, but not that day; I was paralyzed and had no strength to move, let alone run.

When my mother came to the porch, I knew she sensed I was off because the first thing she asked was, "What's wrong with you?" I wanted to scream out what happened, but when I opened my mouth, "nothing's wrong" was all that came out. The only thing I could hear was Jason's voice "if you tell, I will kill all of y'all" echoing within the walls of my head.

Squinting her eyes, mom turned and headed back in the house. I could tell she could feel something was wrong, but I don't think she would have appreciated the answer. I sat on the porch plotting my escape until my mom called me in for dinner. I sat at the table picking over my food. My appetite was completely shot and as good as the meatloaf looked, I didn't feel like eating one bit of it.

"Monique, are you ok?" mom asked.

"Yes, yes, I'm fine."

"You don't seem fine, are you sick?" she felt my head to see if I had a fever, but I shooed her away.

"No." It was then that Jason cleared his throat and cut his eyes at me. "I'm just tired."

"Well finish your dinner so you can get ready for bed." I nodded my head in agreement but I couldn't bring myself to rush, so my mom suggested that I skip dinner and go right to sleep. I glided up the stairs, avoiding eye contact with everyone, but I was still in some sort of a trance that had me shook. I looked at the very spot that Jason took away my innocence and then glared at my bed for a while. Eventually I crawled in it, but I never took off my clothes; I just set up on my bed the whole night trying my best not to go to sleep because I was afraid that if I did, something else might happen to me. There were a few moments when I would slip away into slumber, but every time I did, I would wake up in a cold sweat. I was in and out all night and I didn't really sleep until the next morning when I knew that Jason was gone.

"Are you going to sleep all day?" mom asked me as she casually strolled in my room.

"No."

"Well, get up and get moving", she insisted. I struggled out of bed and inched my way into the kitchen. My stomach was rumbling, but somehow, I didn't feel like eating, so I ate just enough to take away the hunger pains and then I went into the front room to color. I created my own little space on the floor and transported to my own little world. It was the perfect opportunity to lose myself for a while because I certainly didn't want to be *there*. As I kept my mind busy, mom tip toed in the room, watching me as I tried to color my inner sorrow away.

"You are acting pretty weird... are you sure you're ok?" she asked. I lied.

"Uh huh"

"Do you want to go to the store with me?" I shook my head no.

"Well your granddad is here, so 'Queena and I will be back shortly. But when I get back here, were going to talk because it's obvious that something is bothering you." I was happy that she noticed, but what could I say? How could I tell her what was wrong? What was I going to do? All kinds of things were running through my mind, when all of a sudden, a light bulb went off.

I grabbed my crayons and a piece of paper and quickly went to work. It didn't take me long to complete my drawing, and I just knew that it was going to be my ticket out of this misery. I examined the little stick figure girl lying on the floor with big tear drops falling from her face. I then looked at the stick man hovering over her and grimaced at the fact that he hurt her. The red coloring around the girls' bottom area was a nice touch but the icing on the cake was the "don't tell" speech bubble coming from the man. Not long after I finished my picture, my mom came back home.

"Ok little girl, let's talk." I looked at her with so much fear – fear that she would be disappointed in me, fear that she wouldn't love me anymore – not to mention I didn't want to hurt her. Plus, I was used to lying to get my way, so there was a possibility she wouldn't even believe me to begin with. I inched towards her, holding my picture close to my chest, as if the drawings were going to float off of the page and disappear if I didn't protect them. I hesitated to give her the picture, but I *needed* her to know the truth so that she could help me. I took a deep breath and handed her the picture.

"What is this?" she questioned. After only a moment, her eyes went wide and I swear, I saw them shimmer in the light as if she was about to burst into tears.

"Is this? Oh my God… Did someone do this to you?"

I nodded my head. "Yes," I whispered to her.

"Wh- Who did this?" mom shrieked. I tried to tell her, but instead, started to shake.

"Monique! Who did this to you?!"

Still trembling, I asked, "If I tell you, are you going to be mad at me?"

"No, absolutely not."

"It…" I began. I paused and looked into mom's eyes. Tears. They were there, sitting on her bottom eyelid and I knew that whatever was going to come out of my mouth next was going to initiate the waterworks. But I had to. I just couldn't bare the secret anymore.

"… it was Jason."

"Oh God! Oh God!" mom cried out. Her heart was so heavy, she buried her head in her hands and wept.

"Mom, he said that if I told you that he would kill all of us," I explained to her. It was *that* phrase that sent her bouncing out of her seat, tears still in her eyes. She grabbed the phone and rung my grandmother. I didn't know what she said to her in that moment, but it must've been to leave that house immediately because that's what we did. My mom packed us a small bag and dragged my sister and me out of the house and straight to a shelter that reminded me of where we stayed when Jason kicked us out. I *still* didn't want to go there because everyone would have to sleep in the same room, but oddly enough, I knew I would feel safer there.

The nighttime appeared to pass by quickly and morning was staring me in the face. Before long, we were eating breakfast with the other homeless people and planned to head back to the house to pack the rest of our clothes. We waited a while so that we didn't run into Jason.

"Go get your stuff," mom told me as we entered the empty house. I nodded and scurried up to my room to pack up my stuff. With my overfilled backpack in tow, I headed back towards the front door, but noticed something strange. The only bags that were at the door were mine...

CHAPTER TWO

Not too long after we got back to the house, my grandmother arrived along with my uncles to pick us up.

"Pippi, are you ok?!" grandmother asked me, as she engulfed me in a huge embrace. I hugged her back, and before I could answer, she began screaming.

"Where's that no-good son-of-a bi**h Jason at?"

"He's not here," mom said.

After pacing the floor for a few moments, my uncles Leon and Marcus began loading up the car. They only put my bags in the trunk and when they shut it, I realized then that my mom and 'Queena were not coming with us. Mom was just going to let me go.

I knew it! She doesn't love me anymore. I guess its official – she hates me, I thought to myself. She must have forgotten that Jason said that he was going to kill them too – that would have been enough for me to pack up everything I owned and hit the road, but I didn't ask questions.

"If he comes home before we leave, I'll do the shooting and ya'll do the driving," grandmom told Leon and Marcus. They nodded their heads and even chuckled at the idea, but it was clear that grandmom was livid and came for war.

Come on Jason, come on! I chanted in my head. I wanted him to come home so bad. Seeing my grandmom chase him around the house, putting holes in the walls and eventually in him sounded good to me.

Well, Jason got lucky. He never came home, and it would have given grandmom great joy to give him what was coming to him, but she was also anxious to head back down the road. With tears in my eyes, I hugged and kissed my mom and 'Queena goodbye. I didn't want to leave them behind because I was sure that Jason was going to make good on his promise to me. But leaving them behind was the safest thing for me.

We left the house of pain, and to my disappointment there was no shooting involved. After hours and hours of my uncles and grandmother driving, I was home again in Upland. We arrived in the wee hours of the morning and everyone in the house was asleep, so it was not until morning that my aunts Stacy and Juanita greeted me. For a while things were a *little* weird.

No one picked on me, not even my uncle Marcus, who loved messing with me. It seemed like even Sheba had forgotten who I was. I think that everyone felt sorry for me. They didn't know how to treat me, so they kind of left me alone.

A couple of weeks went by and my uncle Marcus must have noticed that I was sad because he started picking with me again, which was a joy for me because all I wanted was to be okay and feel normal. The sun was coming out and ice finally began to break again.

During the year and a half that I was gone, most of my neighborhood friends had moved away – all expect for Natasha and Eliza, two sisters who lived two houses away from my grandmom.

When I went to their house a few days after moving back, Janise, one of their older sisters, opened the door.

"Hey, how are you? Are you visiting?" she greeted.

"No, I moved back here with my grandmom. Are Natasha and Eliza home?"

"Oh yeah, they're here," she nodded. With a smile, she hollered, "Tasha and Liza you have company!" In no time, the two of them came tumbling down the steps, rushing the door. When they saw that it was me, both of their eyes lit up.

"*Hey! What's up?!*" they both said in unison as they extended their arms to hug me. We sat down and began catching up and I swear they must have asked me a million and one questions. "*Where did you go? Did you like the school? Did you have a lot of friends? Didn't your mom have a baby? What did she have?*" The questions went on and on, but I didn't mind; I was just happy to see them. In all the commotion, Liza managed to build up a thirst that just had to be quenched in the middle of my interrogation, so we all headed towards the kitchen where their brother, Kenny, was sitting.

"Hey sweetness", he said in a soft but masculine whisper.

"Hey Ken", I replied with a smirk. Tasha rolled her eyes. "Ken don't start. Moe's not here for you."

"Yeah, I know," Ken responded, making a sour face at her. "I'm about to leave anyway." He looked at me and said "I'll catch ya later," as he winked. Ken was a few years older than Tasha and Liza, but that did not stop Tasha from being the bossy one and it definitely didn't stop my heart from beating out of control for him.

Liza offered me something to drink, but I didn't hear a word that she said because I was in la la land. I could not believe how *fine* Ken was – don't get me wrong he was never ugly, but before he was just cute.

"Girl snap out of it!" Tasha insisted. I let the thoughts that ran in my mind stay in my mind as Tasha, Liza, and I continued catching up, gossiping, and carrying on until dusk.

Things could not get any better for me. I was in a loving environment surrounded by friends and family who loved me, I was safe, I had a great home, was eating good, I had nice clothes and did I mention that I was safe?

A little less than a month later, I started school at Main Street Elementary. The school year had already started, so I was the "new kid". I felt completely out of place - I didn't like my teacher, Ms. Walker, I didn't like the classroom, I didn't like the lunchroom, I just did not like the school at all. It was a bit of a downgrade from what I was accustomed to in Georgia, but I was going to have to adjust.

I couldn't wait for the weekends, so I could get a break from the whole school scene. I would often go with my cousins to stay with their father, whose name was Lewis, for the weekend. Their father was like an uncle to me because he used to live with us before him and my aunt Stacy broke up.

There was one particular Friday that I remember so well. We went to McDonalds for dinner, had ice cream for dessert, played Centipede on the Atari and then we watched a movie. That was such a good day and was truly the highlight of my week. When we woke up that Saturday, we had a big home-cooked breakfast then we went to the neighborhood playground, to the movies, and we later had pizza. By the time we got home, we were all exhausted, but my cousins fell asleep early, while I continued running off the little bit of energy I had left. In the midst of the fun I was having by myself, I developed a sudden craving for ice cream, so I went looking for Uncle Lewis, hoping he would spoil me with a scoop or two.

"Uncle Lewis, could I have some ice cream please?" I asked him as he sat on his bed. A friendly grin flashed across his face.

"Sure," he said, "but will you watch a movie with me?" I shrugged and nodded with a huge toothy smile. Ice cream *and* a movie? It was a no brainer. After I got my ice cream, I went into his room to watch the movie. I was just about finished eating the last of bit of chocolate-y goodness, when the lady on the television took her top off. She danced around some man, who was clearly enjoying himself, and the more she danced, the more clothes she shed. Once she was completely naked, she started taking off the man's clothes and I knew that was my cue to leave.

"The movie's just getting started and you said that you'd watch a movie with me, didn't you?" he mentioned as my hand stayed frozen on the door knob. Before I could answer, he bellowed, "So sit down!"

I sat on the edge of the bed and when I looked at the TV, the man was completely naked and the woman had her head in between his - well you know. I had never seen anything like this before so I was uncomfortable, but a little curious at the same time. Soon, the actors switched positions and Lewis gently pushed me back on the bed. It was at that moment when I knew that he wanted to do to me what Jason had done. I tried getting up because there was no way I wanted to experience that pain again, but Lewis gently lowered me back on the bed.

"Relax. I'm not going to hurt you," he muttered, and well, he was right. He didn't hurt me. I didn't even know what to call what he was doing to me and I certainly didn't know how to respond because it wasn't a good experience, but it wasn't a bad one either. Afterwards, I knew what he did was wrong because he told me that it had to be our secret. I agreed to keep my mouth shut, and after all, who would believe me anyway? Everybody loved him and there was no chance my family was going to accept this. He continued to con me by alluding to the fact that I wouldn't get to see my cousins anymore if I told and it would be all my fault. I believed him. Who would believe that he would do such a thing to me, and better yet, who would care? I promised myself that I wouldn't tell a soul because I didn't want to be the reason why my cousins couldn't see their dad anymore.

The next day when he took us back to grandmom's house, he acted like nothing happened. I figured that I needed to pretend too, but on the inside I was screaming and there was a knot in my stomach that I just couldn't get rid of.

Now, on top of not liking school, I had this extra weight I had to carry. With all that I was going through, I just could not get adjusted, so I began acting out. I was always being sent to the principal's office for talking too much in class, talking back to the teacher, and being disruptive. After my third visit, the principal took out a long wooden paddle.

"Hands against the wall!" he demanded as he proceeded to smack my butt. Sure it hurt, but Mr. Principal was delusional if he thought that a few smacks on the bottom were going to "save me" - in fact, it only made me more determined not to change.

Somewhere in the midst of my mischief, my mom showed up at my grandma's house along with my little sister and moved in. I was really mad at my mom for showing up out of nowhere and pretending like everything was okay. I mean, how could she lay her head next to the man who stole my innocence? I was furious, and to prove a point, I continued to show off in school. It got so bad that nothing Mr. Principal would do could stop me, so the school contacted my mother to report my outrageous behavior.

The next morning was no different than any other. I brushed my teeth, washed my face, and went off to school. No more than five minutes into the school day, I looked up and saw my mom was standing in the classroom doorway. I thought to myself,

What the heck is she doing here? She made eye contact with me, eyes just as blazing as a fiery pit.

"Come here!" she powerfully demanded. I could hear ooos coming from my classmates as all eyes followed me as I inched my way towards her. Before I could even complete my walk of shame, mom grabbed my arm, drug me in front of the class and whooped me right on the spot. It all happened so fast, I didn't even see where the belt came from nor could I process the fact that my classmates and Ms. Walker were completely mortified and embarrassed for me, as was I. Out of breath and out of steam, she released me from her clutches and as she stood there catching her breath I realized I had really messed up.

"If you have any more problems with her, please don't hesitate to call," she calmly stated before leaving the room as I stood there ashamed. Not knowing what else to do, I turned to Ms. Walker, red-eyed and sniffling and murmured, *"Can I be excused?"*

The next day at school, I was greeted with stares and laughs and boy was I embarrassed. I just knew that I couldn't possibly show my face in school again nor did I want to. After that, when it was time for school I would get up, get dressed, eat breakfast, and head out the door. Only, after everyone left for work or school, I would go back to the house. I'd sneak back in through the back sliding door that I kept unlocked and it worked like a charm... for a couple days.

On the third day of cutting school, I went back to the house to discover that someone had locked the door. For a second, I thought about going to school because it was a little cold outside, but I had a flashback of the kids laughing and taunting me, so I decided to stay home. I sat next to Sheba and hugged my legs so I could try and get some sleep, but Sheba just wouldn't let me – not to mention it was so uncomfortable and my butt was starting to get cold. After a while, I couldn't help but get bored; I had drawn a few pictures on some scrap paper from my backpack, scribbled my name so many times, and played with Sheba. There was nothing else for me to do but sit and wait. The next thing I knew, a shadow casted itself over me and when I looked up, it was Kenny.

"What are you doing out of school?" he asked.

"I'm not going back to school!" I replied.

"Why?"

"I just don't like that school." There was no way I was going to tell him that my mom lit my butt up in front of my class and that I was too embarrassed to go back.

"Well aren't you cold," he asked.

"A little…"

"Well you can come over to my house to get warmed up." I couldn't gather my things fast enough. Ken grabbed my book bag, swung it over his shoulder and walked towards his house. When we got to the door, he held it open and let me go in first. *He is fine and a gentleman!* I thought to myself.

"So Ken, how did you know that I was outside," I asked?

"I heard the dog barking a lot as if someone was messing with her so I looked out of the window and saw you. I got dressed and I came out to check on you," he admitted. He walked into the kitchen and began rustling through some dishes. "Moe, make yourself at home and relax. Do you want something to drink?" he asked.

"Uhm, sure!" I took my coat off and glance over at the clock that read 10:20 a.m. I thought that it would have at least been around 1 p.m. - it seemed like I was outside for hours.

"Here you go sweetness," Ken said, handing me a glass of juice.

"Thanks," I acknowledged with a sweet smile.

"You look sleepy," he noted. I wasn't even remotely tired, but for some reason, Ken had me under his spell and it seemed like anything he said was truth.

I responded, "I am a little," rubbing my eyes.

"Well you can lie down if you want to." I stared at him and nodded okay, to which Ken then reached out his hand to mine and said, "Come on". We headed upstairs towards his room.

"Go ahead lay down", he insisted and like a fool, I did. He turned on the television and sat on the edge of the bed. I laid my head down despite feeling wide awake, but after about 25 minutes, I managed to drift off to sleep. I hadn't yet gone deep enough into sleep to not notice Ken making himself comfortable as he laid next to me. His breathing was steady and quiet and I could feel the warmth of his breath on the back of my neck as he slowly put his arm around my waist. My eyes popped open; I inhaled and exhaled a few times as I began to get uneasy. Vivid thoughts of Jason on top of me caused me to quiver.

"Chill, I am not going to hurt you," Ken whispered to me. Those words calmed me down, but only a little bit. He turned me towards him and asked, "Have you ever kissed a boy before?"

"No," I shamelessly admitted.

"I can be your first, if you want me to?" he asserted.

The idea of him asking for my permission instead of being forceful made me believe that he was nothing like Jason. He asked, so he must have cared if I wanted it. That was the quickest shut down my guard had ever had.

"Sure," I agreed. Ken lifted my chin and placed his lips on mine moving his lips back and forth. I noticed his eyes were closed so I closed mine too - he even put his hand on my butt and squeezed it, but that was it. Nothing else happened except for us falling asleep. Ken kept his word by not hurting me and that meant the world to me. I couldn't help but think that I was in love.

Soon it was time for me to go home, but before I left Ken's house, he urged me not to tell anyone what had happened, especially not my uncle Marcus.

"If someone finds out you were here instead of school, you will never be able to stay here again," he explained. I didn't have to think through that reasoning too much; that was a good reason for me not to say a word, so I left his house and went to mine pretending like I had such a good day in school.

The next morning, I got up and actually decided to go back to school. When I walked into my classroom, Ms. Walker said, "Welcome back, I'm glad to see that you're better." It hadn't dawned on me that I was going to need an actual excuse for missing three days of school up until that moment, but it seemed as though I didn't need to make one up. I smiled and thanked her before taking my seat. I was a bit confused, but I knew it wouldn't be wise to ask any questions.

I made sure to not give my teacher a reason to call my mom, so I was on my best behavior all day. It was also nice not to be ridiculed about getting my butt beat in front of everyone. From that day on, things started to change for me for the better. Class became more enjoyable and I had a newfound appreciation for Ms. Walker and other things about the school that I previously hated. Ms. Walker was so impressed by how much my behavior improved that she gave me a certificate that read "YOU DID IT!"

I was over Liza and Tasha's house almost every day, and most the time Ken was there or he would come in the house before I left to go home for dinner. He would blow me kisses if there were other people around, but when they weren't he would give me an actual kiss. The secret rendezvouses went on for months and I even would cut school to go over Ken's house once in a while. Somehow, no one ever found out about it, but when the summer came, I didn't see much of him. He had a day job and most of the time there was always someone else at either of our houses, so meeting up was harder to do.

The summer I turned 10, my mom decided it was time to move again. That was fine for me because I had plans on staying right where I was. Liza was outside playing so I went outside to tell her that my mom was moving and in the midst of our conversation, I saw Ken coming out of the house hugged up with some other girl. I was instantly crushed, and though that very sight hurt me, my world came crashing down when he failed to even acknowledge my presence. My heart fell down to my toes and all I could do in that moment was run off crying. It only took me few minutes of shedding tears before I decided to move with my mom. All of the love that I thought I had for Kenny was squashed and I never wanted to see him again. Moving would definitely be the best way for my broken heart to heal.

CHAPTER THREE

Anticipating the move was like waiting for Christmas to come in July; it took forever, but moving day eventually came and I had all my things packed and ready to go. We were moving to North Philadelphia to live with my maternal grandfather. I was not sure how things were going to work out because I never had a real relationship with my grandfather; I knew his name was the same as Ken's and that he was a preacher, but I didn't know much of anything else.

The house was spacious with three bedrooms and one bath. My sister and I shared a room which had a door that led to my grand pop's room and my mom had her own bedroom. It took about a week and a half for me to unpack my things, but it took my mom forever to unpack her belongings.

Soon after settling in, I got the urge to get out of the house, so I asked my mom if I could go outside and play.

"Sure," she replied. "But stay on this block." I assured her I would and since I didn't know anyone anyway, there wasn't a reason for me to venture too far. I took a few toys outside on the front porch to play with and it must have looked like I was having so much fun because soon enough two girls popped up out of nowhere.

"Hi, my name is Pam. What's your name?" One of them asked while the other followed up with, "Are you new around here?" After I told them that I had just moved in a couple of weeks ago, Pam asked if I wanted to play with them. I didn't see the harm so I agreed, plus if I was having fun on my own, I was for sure going to have fun with two more people. We all shared introductions and needless to say, Pam, Erica, and I instantly became friends. We three played together for the rest of the summer and when school started we would walk to and from school together. We were like three peas in a pod.

One day on our way to school, I noticed that Erica was not quite herself. I asked her numerous times what was wrong with her but she kept saying nothing. Pam ended up going home early because she was sick, so after school it was just me and Erica. As we approached our block Erica asked, "Can I trust you?"

"Sure, why ya ask?"

She looked around as if to make sure no one else was close enough to hear. "If I tell you what's wrong, don't tell anyone else, okay?"

I nodded. "Okay." Erica took a deep breath and looked me straight in my eyes. I knew whatever she was about to tell me was serious.

"I am afraid to go home 'cause my daddy abused me last night."

"What? What he do?"

"He smacked me in the face and then he took a hanger and smacked me again." Shock washed across my face as I tried to find the right words to say.

"What did your mom say?" I inquired. Erica's eyes shifted to the ground.

"Nothing."

My thoughts raced in my mind. I tried to figure out what to say to comfort her but before my brain could make sense of anything, I blurted out my own truth.

"I was abused too." I'm not sure why I said that. Perhaps to make her feel better, or even in a weird way, to make myself feel better, but it felt kind of good to let it out anyway. We exchanged stares, and though we were silent, I could tell she understood me and she knew I understood her. I continued to ramble, telling her what had happened to me. The more I spoke, the more emotional we became, but I could feel the weights lifting off my shoulders with every word that came out of my mouth. By the time I was done, there were so many tears shed, that we had stopped walking, oddly enough in front of an abandoned house. As people passed us on the street, they shot us odd and confused looks, but their stares didn't faze us at all. We soon got ourselves together and headed back home. I encouraged Erica by telling her if she prayed, God will take her dad away just like he did Jason.

"What happen to him, did he die?" she asked.

"No."

"Did he go to jail?"

"No."

"Well how did he go away then?"

"I don't know. I guess I mean that I just didn't have to be around him anymore." By this time, we were in front of our doorsteps, so we hugged goodbye and stayed in for the rest of the night. The next day, Erica came to my house before school. Pam was still sick, so it was just her, but she arrived in a strangely chipper mood.

"It worked!" she exclaimed.

"What worked?" I asked a bit confused.

"The prayer! My dad punched my mom in the eye and she called the police! When the police came to the house they took my dad with them, so you see it worked!" She explained as she engulfed me in an excited embrace. I was happy for her, but I would be lying if I said I wasn't surprised that what I had told her to do worked – at least so quickly anyway.

Within that same week, I was sitting in my room looking at television when the doorbell rang. It rang a few times and it was obvious that they weren't going away, so I rushed to the door.

"Open the door!" mom yelled out of her room. I rolled my eyes because I was already on my way, but I put some pep in my step and made it to the door before it could ring again. It only took one second for the whole world around me to stop. My eyes widened and my gaze zeroed in on the familiar and scary eyes that met mine. I could feel myself reacting in slow motion as I examined the person in front of me from head to toe not believing my own eyes that I could be possibly looking at the person that began the snowball that was my ruined childhood.

Jason stared down at me, without so much as a smile, a hello, or even a blink as I stumbled backwards.

He's here to kill us! I thought to myself. My heart palpitated and if any more time had passed, I might have had a heart attack. Before I could shout out, my mom was standing behind me. I turned to her and noticed she had on her nice blouse and looked like she was ready for a night out.

"Alright Monique, I'm going out for a few hours. I'll be back," she said as she walked hand in hand with the monster from my past. I couldn't believe I was watching them both *together* with my own eyes. There was no way that my mom was really going out with the maniac that took advantage of me. I *still* couldn't shake the nightmares. My eyes were filled with tears as I ran to my room and slammed the door. I grabbed a teddy bear and crawled into a corner. Angry, sickened, and heartbroken, I had no choice but to accept it and watch mom go off on a date with that snake. As I cuddled my teddy bear tight, I thought maybe my prayer expired or something. I mean, what did I do now that Jason had suddenly appeared out of nowhere? Perhaps it didn't occur to her that I would be upset... or maybe she just didn't care. After giving that sentiment some thought, I figured it was Jason that she cared about the most. I fell asleep in that corner and when I woke up the next morning, I went to the hallway to see if my mom was back home, but her bedroom door was shut.

My mom continued to see Jason on a regular basis, and not once did he say that he was sorry for what he had done to me or my mom. Hatred boiled up so much inside of me that I did the only thing I thought I could do: figure out how to kill him.

One night, mom said to me, "Monique get yourself together, we're going out for dinner." At this point I was still distant with her, so I silently did what she asked. We headed towards the Chinese restaurant, which was two blocks away from where we lived, so I thought that we were going there to get dinner and I even got a little excited. I became utterly confused when we passed the Chinese restaurant and turned up the street, but I just followed my mom without saying a word.

We strolled up to a house that was in the middle of that block. I had no idea whose house we were at, but mom confidently rang the doorbell, so she most definitely knew.

"Come in," a woman, who looked vaguely familiar greeted us at the door. She took our coats and led us into the dining room where she invited us to have a seat. A young boy around my age approached the table to sit and the woman whose name is Mrs. Paula instructed the young boy to introduce himself.

"Hi, I'm Don," he said. Mrs. Paula gave the boy a look of approval and then roared, "Come on ya'll, it's time for dinner!"

One man, who was very big and sported an afro, came out of the kitchen with a plate already in his hand and Jason came down the steps. When I saw him my heart skipped several beats. It felt like I was about to die, and in that moment, I wouldn't have minded. How could my life possibly get any worse? Now without any choice, I had to sit and eat dinner with him and these strange people.

I didn't eat my food - I sort of picked over it. I was looking around at everyone being so happy and deep into conversation with one another and tears began to fill my eyes. I continued to fight back the waterworks and a panic attack throughout the entire dinner, and somehow, someway I managed to make it through that evening.

A couple days later, Mrs. Paula sent this tall, light-skinned woman named Betty to our house. She was a Jehovah's Witness and she was there to have bible study with me and my mom. Sister Betty had given us a Watchtower, a pamphlet with Jehovah's Witness literature in it, which reminded me of a comic book without the laughs. That lesson was one of the longest lessons that I was ever taught and I *still* don't even remember anything that she said. Sister Betty started coming on a weekly basis for bible study and before long, she began encouraging my mom to attend a service at the Kingdom Hall. The Kingdom Hall was like sitting in a dark dungeon with no hope of ever seeing the light of day. It was so boring and it didn't help that when they sang, they sounded lifeless and more bored than I was. The preaching was no better - I felt like I was in the most spiritless service ever. *When was Jehovah going to show up?* I thought to myself all service.

I sat next to my mom and ''Queena wondering how someone could confess salvation and still do sinful things. No one had to tell me that drinking and smoking was wrong - I knew that for myself. What I didn't know was why it was okay for someone to say that they were a Jehovah's Witness and still do those things? Even at 10 years old, I wanted to know what religion God was really a part of. I went on a mission to find out which religion I thought would be best for me. I decided to take the Holy Bible and compare it with the books from other religions.

First, I started with the two religions I had been exposed to since we were living in the same house. In my opinion, God could not be in the Jehovah's Witness religion because why would He give you life and not want you to acknowledge your birthday or any other holiday? Also, people of that faith partied and told me that Hell was here on Earth and that just didn't sit right with me. Even though there were many times that I felt like I was living in Hell, I still knew better. I also remembered the morning that I woke up with a terrible headache and my grandfather came into the room, prayed for me in the name of Jesus, and my headache disappeared. I was impressed with how every time I or someone prayed in the name of Jesus how the situation would seem to turn around. Even though I wasn't sure how my prayer about Jason backfired, I still had high hopes that just saying Jesus' name worked wonders.

Just when I thought that I had discovered the religion that was right for me, I made a shocking discovery. I went to the fridge for a snack and notice a six pack of beer. I saw my mom drink before but never that kind of alcohol so I did not think it was hers. Come to find out, the beer belonged to my grandfather.

"Why are you drinking beer? I thought you couldn't do that since you go to church?"

"I'm trying to gain weight. It's nothing to worry about," he stated seriously. I didn't approve of his answer and just as quick as I thought I found what I was looking for, I was right back at square one, but this time, with no sense of direction. I decided to ask a Muslim girl at school named Kareema about her belief system.

"So, what do ya'll do?" I asked her.

"Well, we have prayer a lot," she explained. My interest peaked and when I asked for more, she explained she prayed to a guy named Muhammad. I paused and thought, *Huh? Who is Muhammad?* No better way to find out than to see for myself. When I walked into her house, there were miniature candles everywhere, and on the floor were big pillows that we had to kneel on to pray. Her father introduced himself and placed a kufi hat on his head that reminded me of an old sock. Her father began to pray in the name of Allah and I became confused. What about that Muhammed guy? After prayer, I questioned her father as to who Allah was. He told me that Allah was a man who is their God. I did not think that a man who was flesh and blood like me could really be God, so I decided Islam was not for me. I thought to myself, what else is there? Then I remembered Ashley. At lunch, I asked her to enlighten me about Catholicism.

She told me that they pray to the Virgin Mary and recite "Hail Mary full of grace" as you make a cross sign across your chest. If you sinned, there was a priest in a booth that you had to confess your sins to. A man and a statue? I just didn't think that God was a statue, and why, if I sinned would God have me to confess to a man?

After all that hunting I did for guidance, I came up dry, so I decided that Christianity would be the best for me. Not that I was going to be a devout Christian right then and there - I was only ten and a half years old and had a lot more to learn and a lot more mistakes to make.

After I came to that realization, it was as if all hell had broken loose. I couldn't sleep because it was as if I was being tormented with demons that looked like Jason and they were all trying to kill me. My nose started bleeding on a regular basis, my stomach was in knots and my little boobies begin to hurt. After about a week of this unusual behavior, I couldn't take it anymore. I locked myself in a bathroom stall at school and noticed blood in my underwear. I was terrified because the only time I had bled like that was when Jason forced himself on me. I was frozen and didn't know what to do, so I just sat on the toilet, aching, afraid, and just wishing that all the pain would go away.

I was probably in the bathroom too long because my teacher sent one of my classmates in to get me. I ended up going to the nurse, who called my mom to come and pick me up. As my mom and I walked home, she started to explain what was actually going on with me.

Half of me was disgusted because the bleeding only brought back memories, but the other half of me was relieved to know that I was't the only one that had to go through that. When I found out that I would have a period every month, I couldn't help but be angry with God because now I was going to have a constant reminder of what Jason did to me.

CHAPTER FOUR

A new school year arrived, and I was a little nervous because it was my first time riding a bus to a school that was really far from home. The ride alone was about 45 minutes and not to mention I was leaving my friends behind. I wasn't too worried about making new ones though because that was never hard for me to do.

On the first day of school it was as if I was invisible; no one spoke to me except for the teacher. I told myself that I was not going to try too hard to fit in with the other kids, but after about two weeks of being isolated, I had to come up with some sort of plan to make this school situation work for me. Each day at lunch time, I noticed that the person that had the most candy seemed to be the one that had the most friends. A light bulb went off in my head, and I knew what I needed to do. One day after school, I asked my mom for money to buy school supplies from the school store. Of course, I lied because she definitely wouldn't have given me money for candy to impress a bunch of stuck up fifth graders. She handed me two quarters. I held them in my hand half expecting for her to rummage in her wallet for more, but when I saw her put her pocketbook up, I realized that was all she was planning on giving me. Now, just what did she expect me to do with that? I needed more money if I was going to impress those kids, but where was I going to get more money from? I thanked mom for her generosity in the most sarcastic way possible without getting popped in the head for being smart and walked away, pondering how I was going to come up with the rest of the cash.

"Bingo!" I said to myself. I remembered peeking in on my grandfather one day as he was counting money and when he was done, he placed it in his dresser drawer. I snuck into his room from the door that led from my room to his. Slowly and quietly, I opened the dresser and presto! There was the envelope. It had the date and some other writing on it, but in the envelope was a lot of money and some checks that had the name of my grandfather's church on it. I was shocked to think that he would steal money from his own church, but shucks, it made me feel less guilty about stealing from him. Without any more delay, I pulled out a twenty-dollar bill, closed the envelope, shut the drawer and left the room.

I stashed the cash in my bookbag and laid on my bed and started to do my homework as I normally did. Everything was fine until later that evening when my grandfather came home from work. I started to get a little uneasy, but it was all for nothing because my grand pop didn't notice a thing.

I woke up the next morning with a new attitude. I had a mission to accomplish, and I had the ammunition I needed to get the job done. Entering the school yard that morning was no different than any other morning - I was still invisible. However, I was confident that that would be the last time that would happen. The clock on the wall was all I really focused on in class and when 11:45 a.m. came, I knew I was only minutes from becoming popular.

After entering the lunchroom, I quickly checked my pocket to make sure that the money was still in there. A huge grin spread across my face when I pulled that crisp $20 bill out of my pocket. I wanted to wave it around as if it were a golden ticket or something, but I kept control. Immediately following lunch, I went to the school store and spent every penny on Peanut Swirls, Now and Laters, Lemon Heads, Chews, and bubble gum. In spite of the faces that the cashier made, she never asked any questions. I walked out of that store with over 400 pieces of candy.

I eagerly walked back into the lunchroom for the next shift, found a seat in the corner, and dumped out all the goodies. Another smile crept across my face as I watched all eyes suddenly turn to me and just as I thought, my classmates could not resist. Hook, line, and sinker. Kids and questions were coming from so many ways, I couldn't figure out where to start.

"Where did you get all this from? How did you get all this candy? Did you steal this candy?" They all came at me, but I tamed the situation. I ended up giving about eight kids some candy and turned away the others. I had to be smart about the situation - after all, I had to keep a stash for as long as I could.

Everything was going according to my plan, but after about two weeks, my candy supply started to dwindle. Inevitably, I had to keep raiding my grandfather's drawer in order to replenish my candy supply. As my relationships started to develop with my new friends, so did my mom's relationship with Jason. I felt like a ship that was sinking slowly with no help in sight.

CHAPTER FIVE

I decided not to let my past situation with Jason hinder my future, so I told myself not to care about what him and my mom were doing – I would just pretend not to notice with the hopes that Jason wouldn't notice me. Just when it seemed like I was completely invisible, Jason came up behind me and rubbed up against me. I froze and shuddered as he whispered to me, "Boy, aren't you growing up." I should have known better than to think that ignoring him would really work. Every bone in my body began to shake as flashbacks of the past played out right in front of me.

I watched my mom bounce down the steps all cheerful, not having a clue as to what just happened. *Tell her,* one part of me said while the other part of me retorted *she don't care anyway,* so I kept it to myself. I felt rage build up in me. I could see myself killing him, stabbing him repeatedly as blood splattered everywhere.

"I wanna play," 'Queena said, snapping me out of my zone.

71

Annoyed, I growled, "Well I don't!" and stormed off.

When I went back to school, I was mad with everyone around me and I wanted to be alone. I wouldn't have minded being invisible again, but just my luck - I was now popular and people were all up in my face laughing, talking and getting on my nerves on the one day I needed space.

"What's wrong with you?" one girl asked me. I just cut my eyes at her and frowned. "You're acting weird," Welp, you know me - I could not let that slide.

"And you look weird!" I responded. Everyone around me, including her, was stunned, though they did manage to snicker at the girl's expense.

"Well we'll see about that", she said before shuffling away.

I did a good job of isolating myself the whole morning and was looking forward to continuing my day that way. Lunch time came and children huddled around me like I was their candy ATM. I couldn't take it – all the begging and babbling about nothing was too much.

"Leave me alone!" I screamed. And they did. They walked away looking puzzled. After lunch, we headed out into the play yard for recess. Some of the kids decided to play kickball and the same girl who told me that I was acting weird earlier that day kicked the ball directly at me. I glared at her and noticed she had a smirk on her face. Since she thought she was being funny and cute, I decided to show her how I felt. I strolled right up to her with my fist balled and punched her square in the face. Shock and pain washed across her face as she stared at me wide-eyed before she swung on me.

"Oh! They fighting!" I heard one of the boys say.

We started scraping and I had her all to myself until a few other kids jumped in to defend her. I took the hits like a champ, but when I saw the blood seeping from my nose, I turned into a lunatic. My arms flailed as I managed to fend off the gang of girls one by one. A girl named Trina came over and started pulling girls off of me, and soon a teacher followed after her screaming, "Break it up! Break it up!"

I managed to get a few more hits in before letting them off the hook. I stood in front of my classmates breathing heavily, while the others had to catch their breaths. I was ready for round two, but as soon as I felt more blood drop from my nose, I backed down.

"Alright, it's over! There's nothing to see here!" the teacher shooed off the gathered students. They all slowly dispersed and went back to doing what they were doing. "Trina, take her to the nurse."

"Okay," she agreed. "Come on," she said as she guided me to the health center. I had seen Trina around every now and then, but had never met her – never even said two words to the girl, so it struck me as odd that she jumped in to the brawl.

"Why did you help me?" I asked holding my nose to keep the blood from leaking.

"'Cause you needed help!" We both giggled and from that day on, we were the best of friends. Becoming friends with Trina was a blessing in disguise. I didn't have to bottle everything inside anymore. I was able to cry on her shoulder and share with her all my hurt and all my fears. I would stay over her house all the time, but I never let her stay with me - I guess because I wanted to be away from home as such as I could.

One day after school, as soon as I went into the house, I heard my grandfather talking really loud. He discovered that "someone" was taking money out of the church envelopes. What he didn't know was that the "someone" was me, or maybe he did but he never accused me. It was a good thing that I had a friend in school now, because I would have sure lost those who were being my friend because of the candy.

The school year was just about over when Jason said to me that he wanted to feel inside of me again.

"Real soon," he smirked. His very presence was unwanted, but whenever he looked at me, I wanted to puke in my mouth. When I told Trina what he said, she told me that I had to tell my mom, but what was she going to do? I told her once and not only did she stay with him, but she sent *me* away. I guess she called herself getting rid of the problem – me.

A week or so went by before I had mustered up enough nerve to say something to my mom. Well as luck would have it, I did not have to do or say anything, because my mom had met another guy. Apparently she had been seeing him for quite some time but didn't want to bring him around my sister and me until she was sure about him. As for Jason, he just kind of disappeared.

Things between my mom and her new friend were getting serious because we were moving to Chester to live with him. He was the total opposite of Jason - he was a nice guy and seemed to be normal. They later married, and my sister and I had a new daddy.

Even though I moved from Philly to Chester, Trina and I still remained close friends. We would call each other all the time, so she knew everything that was going on with me and vice versa. Soon, I started school and I immediately clung to the wrong group of girls.

I went to Pulaski Middle School, where the people were straight from the hood. I had to put on a "tough guy" act just so I wouldn't stand out too much. I got into so much trouble trying to fit in with the crowd. The crazy thing about it was I really didn't like any of the girls. We would jump people for the dumbest reasons - like one day, we fought a girl because she wouldn't do one of the crew's homework. A teacher broke up the fight and we all were sent to the office. One by one, each girl went in to talk with the principal and when it was my turn, I sat in the chair as if I didn't have a care in the world.

"Sit up straight and look at me eye to eye," Mrs. Brown, the principal, demanded. I slowly pulled myself up and looked at her.

"Why are you hanging with girls that are not hanging with you?" she asked. I was speechless. I had no idea what she was talking about and she knew it.

"These girls are not your friends," she began. "They are using you because they know that they can. You, my dear, are different and you have to know your worth." I sat in front of her as her eyes concentrated on me, while mine stayed towards the floor. Her words hit me hard, and though I didn't want to hear them, I knew she was right.

"I'm giving you three days suspension to see if you can figure it out."

She gave me the slip and I got up, left her office, and headed to in-school detention. I thought about what Mrs. Brown said for a couple of days and I began to rationalize why I was the way I was. Of course, I felt like nothing, but I didn't want to live the rest of my life as nothing. I decided not to hang with the crew anymore, not that we did much of that outside of school anyways. I only clung to them because everyone was afraid of them. If you messed with one of them, then you have messed with all of them.

I was tired of getting in trouble; I was always in trouble in school and I was always in trouble at home. I was tired of everything. I was crying out for help but no one seemed to hear me. My mom was so in tune with her life and her husband that she couldn't hear me crying. I was begging for her to love me, but why couldn't she see that I would do things just to get her to pay attention to me?

One night she just started screaming and hollering at me – I can't really tell you why, it could have been for anything. she grabbed an extension cord to beat me, and I told her that I was going to run away. She looked at me and said "don't run, walk."

I did just that.

When I left the house, I had no idea how I was going to survive or where I was going to go. I met up with some kids from the neighborhood and they led me to an abandoned house. When we walked in, I knew that this wasn't the first time that they had been there. There were flash lights, a little radio, and blankets on the floor. It wasn't long before people began to leave, but I was in no rush because I had no place to go. I ended up hanging out with two boys, who were a year or two older; one's nickname was Onion and the other was Rick, who I liked a lot.

"Why don't you show Rick how much you like him? I'd bet he'll like you then," Onion insisted. I was conflicted. On the one hand, I liked Rick and wanted him to like me back. But... I didn't *really* want to be with him like that. Was being with him going to make him give me more attention? If it was, I was willing to do what it took. So, we slept together while Onion and a couple others watched. Then they ran a train on me. I couldn't even tell you where the other two guys came from or who they were. I was screaming and trying my best to fight, but one guy was holding my arms and the other two were holding my legs while one was raping me and that went on for what seemed like a good hour.

I was twelve years old and it was the first time that I willingly had sex with a boy, only to wind up getting violated again. They were laughing and joking and when they had enough of me, they left me there all alone. I cried uncontrollably as I gathered my clothes and got out of there before they came back for another round.

As I was leaving my neighborhood, I saw my stepfather's car driving really slow down the street. I figured he was looking for me, so I ducked down behind a parked car until he was gone, tears still managing to seamlessly stream down my face. I wondered around the streets of Chester for hours before getting tired. There were no people outside, all the stores were closed and it was just me. I ended up at Memorial Park, where I laid down on a bench to go to sleep. I soon drifted into a light slumber but was startled awake by a noise, so I got up and started wandering again. Tired, cold, and hungry, I finally decided to swallow my pride and head home.

I took my time heading home. All the other lights on the block were out – all except Onion's house. I thought to knock on his door and tell his mom what her son did to me and maybe I could get something to eat while there. I finally mustered up enough courage to knock on the door, and when I did, his sister answered and invited me in. She didn't ask me why I was there so late or anything. As I walked in, I could hear music playing in the back.

"Go on back, they're back there," Onion's sister insisted.

I trekked to the back room and lo' and behold, they were having a party. How in the world could he be partying after what he had done to me? To my surprise, I didn't see any of the guys there other than Onion, and when he spotted me, he called me to the side.

"Whatcha doing here?" he asked.

"I have nowhere else to go. After what y'all did to me I couldn't go home. My mom would have known that something had had happened to me and would've called the police on you." Of course that wasn't true, but he didn't know that.

"I'm sorry for how it all went down. If you need to, you can crash here for the night." At first I was going to decline because he wasn't really sorry, and figured he might try it again, but since his sister was there and I needed a place to stay, I agreed. After grabbing some snacks, I climbed into a corner and went to sleep, noise and all.

I was awakened by a loud knock at the door. When Onion's sister answered it, two police officers stood there asking for my whereabouts. Onion's sister didn't hesitate – she led them right to me.

"Young lady, come with us." I willingly got up to leave, and as I was leaving, I looked over at Onion and his face was beet red, which was very odd considering he was normally as black as a boot. He was scared to death that I was going to tell the police what he and his friends had done to me. However, that was not the first thing on my mind because I didn't even know what was going to happen with *me*.

I got into the police car not knowing what was going on. Nothing was said to me nor did I ask questions, but when I looked up, I was home. They walked me into the house to talk with me and my mom. They began to tell me how lucky I was for being found alive, and how there were hundreds of children that ran away from home and never returned, so on and so on. Before they left, they gave me a warning that if I were to ever run away again, I would be sent to juvie if they found me.

"Well, how did you find me this time?" I asked

"We showed your picture around and someone recognized you from the party you were at," one officer said.

The other officer interjected, "Yeah, but next time we might not be that lucky."

My mom never asked where I was or who I was with. I mean she knew what the police told her, but she never asked me for herself. I would have loved to curl up in her arms and cry. I don't know if I would have told her that a bunch of guys took turns on top of me, but I would have told her how scared I was of being out on my own in the park. Knowing her, she would have said "well you shouldn't have been trying to be grown," or something like that.

Shockingly, my stepfather was genuinely concerned about where I was. I guess I just didn't expect it. He told me that he was out for hours looking for me, but I dared not tell him that I saw him. I believe he was the reason the police went looking for me in the first place and it was that day that I started to view my stepfather differently. He was no longer just some man my mom was with; he genuinely cared about my mom, my sister *and* me. Maybe he *could* be a father to me. He had no children of his own so maybe, just maybe, he was sent to me as an angel.

CHAPTER SIX

Weeks went by and my stepfather started spending more time with my sister and me than ever before. It was remarkable; I found myself smiling for no reason at all and I think it was because here was a man that was fulfilling the role of my father and not wanting anything in return.

He became the mediator between my mother and I - I guess he was trying to keep the drama down in the house and for a while it worked.

One Monday morning, I woke up in sweats and there was a sour taste in my mouth. In the pit of my stomach I felt a heaviness I could not explain but I shook it off and started to get ready for school.

Not long after I got to school, a girl named Crystal came up to me.

"Where were you?"

"What?" I replied.

"The wedding. I didn't see you there."

I stared intensely at Crystal, trying to make sense of what she was telling me. "Who's wedding?"

"Your dad's," she said. I paused for a moment and knew that if I showed how I felt in that moment, I would regret it. That feeling I felt earlier started to creep back. I quickly responded, "Oh whatever, I didn't wanna go," and swiftly walked away. I scurried to the bathroom, threw my books on the floor, and bawled. I didn't know my dad was even *getting* married, let alone *already* married. How could he possibly get married to a woman with four kids and wasn't even taking care of me, his only child? How could he get married and not tell me? What made everything worse was that he got married in the same city that I lived in and didn't even invite me.

Am I the only child that has both parents that don't care about me? I thought. I stayed in the bathroom all morning. I probably would have stayed in there all day, but I started to get hungry. I missed my lunch period, so I was in second period lunch eating with the older kids.

Mr. Webster, a substitute teacher for Mrs. Bennett, who was out on maternity leave, noticed me and made a beeline straight for me.

"Why are you in this lunch period?" he asked me. "And why weren't you in class?" I looked up, eyes blood shot red and didn't say a word.

"You've been crying?" he asked. I looked back down and continued to eat my food. "Come on, grab your lunch and come with me."

Great. Just as I thought my day couldn't get any worse, now I was about to be reported for skipping class. Mr. Webster led me into his classroom and told me to take a seat.

"So, what's going on? What has you so upset?"

"Um, nothing's wrong," I lied as I avoided eye contact.

"So nothing is what has you upset?" I hesitantly looked up at him and admired his whole being – he was tall, caramel, and had the most perfect smile. As soon as our eyes met, somehow I felt alright.

"Okay, my dad just got married." He began to comment, but I didn't let him. "Let me tell you how I wasn't invited and how I didn't even know he was getting married. Crystal told me this morning. That's why I'm upset and might I add the lady's four kids were there, but nooooo not me, his only child - no I wasn't there!" By the time I finished ranting, I was in full hysterics and the tears started rushing down. Mr. Webster began to comfort me but the more he consoled me, the more I cried.

"Neither one of my parents really care for me," I admitted. That sentiment took him by surprise, but he didn't interrupt me, he just let me get it all out. I explained how I didn't know what I had done wrong for them not to love me. I mean, don't get me wrong – I acted a fool from time to time but most of the time it was because I wanted attention and it didn't matter whether the attention was positive or negative; I just wanted it. After releasing all my emotions, I calmed down a bit and was starting to feel a tad bit better.

"Would you like for me to be your friend?" Mr. Webster asked me.

"What do you mean?" I responded. It was out of the blue and a bit weird, but I didn't want to read too much into it.

"Well I can be someone for you to talk with and someone for you to depend on", he explained.

Well, that made sense. "Ok, I guess so," I agreed, prompting Mr. Webster to smile.

"Great! It's time for you to go now, but we'll talk again soon."

By the time I left Mr. Webster's class, I was feeling way better – I even managed to smile, though my heart was still hurting.

Weeks went by and I can honestly say that Mr. Webster definitely showed himself to be a friend. He would ask me how I was doing at home, how I was doing in my other classes, how things were with my friends, and so on.

"Monique, I want you to see me after class," he announced one day. The class snickered and I shot them all a look that could kill. When class was over and all the students were gone, he motioned for me to come closer to him. As I approached him, he took off his necklace and put it around my neck.

"This is to remind you of how much I care about you and when we're alone you can call me Eric," he told me as he massaged my shoulders.

I was amazed. "Eric, wow that's your name? Okay, Eric I'll see you later."

As I headed to my next class, I tucked the necklace in my shirt. I was grateful, but a little confused as to why he gave it to me. I mean, it was *real* gold and what if I lost it? I decided not to tell anyone about the necklace because it was kind of weird.

My friends wouldn't understand anyway - they were too immature.

Two days later, Eric and I ate lunch together in his classroom. We talked as usual, but this time I helped him grade papers, which was fun because it made me feel grown up. We ate lunch together the next day as well and Friday he brought me lunch from Two J's, a sandwich shop down the street from the school, but I wanted to be a little show off and decided to eat lunch in the cafeteria again. That was a big mistake. A few girls asked where I had been for the last few lunch periods and since I had nothing to hide, I told them.

"I was with Mr. Webster helping him with papers and stuff."

"Why would he want *you* to help him?" one girl by the name of Asia scuffed.

"Why wouldn't he?" I replied.

Asia smirked. "He wouldn't want you to help him over me! I bet I'll be eating lunch with him next week." I took her up on her bet and the challenge was on, which was another mistake because I spent the entire weekend stressing out about it; I was obsessed with figuring out how to stop Asia from winning. There was no way I could let her take my place. I racked my brain trying to figure out ways to one-up her and finally realized the perfect leverage: the necklace. All I had to do was wear his necklace on the outside of my shirt and Asia would have no choice but to accept that I was better than her and to admit defeat.

While in the middle of conjuring up my master plan, the doorbell rang and guess who it was? My dad and his wife. What in the world were they doing here? What did they want? My mom called me into the living room but I took my sweet time walking in there. I looked at his dark, round face with so much anger I could have burned a hole in his face with my eyes if I had continued to stare at him.

"We're here to talk to you," his wife explained. I rolled my eyes. What could either one of them need to say to me? Then this monkey-looking woman had the nerve to try to initiate conversation. Ugh, I could've done without it all. Despite me wanting to storm out of there, I let them speak. They went on to discuss my behavior and some other crap, but I couldn't tell you what was said because it all went in one ear and out the other. All that talk and nothing was even said about them two getting married. Go figure.

What was funny about the whole situation was the fact that I thought that I was doing good. I hadn't been in any trouble for the last month or so, but regardless, I had bigger fish to fry. Keeping Asia away from Eric was my main priority. I had an idea of what I was going to do, I just needed to finalize a few things.

Monday morning, I woke up ready for war. I left the house looking fresh; tight black jeans, white button down shirt, a black tank top and the icing on the cake - Eric's necklace dangling from my neck.

English was my second period class, so my plan was to ask to go to the bathroom five minutes before my first class let out so that I could be at his class before the bell rang. I guess I got a little nervous because I really did have to use the bathroom, but I still got to his class just as the bell rang for the class change. As soon as all the kids piled out of the room, I went in to put my plan into full effect. Eric saw me and his eyes lit up.

"You do wear it! I've never seen it on you before and you're wearing it well, might I add," he said, speaking about the necklace.

I sighed. "Yeah I really needed to feel you close to me this weekend," I said as I ran my thumb across the gold. My classmates started trickling in, so I quickly asked, "Can we do lunch to talk?"

"Sure", he replied. I quickly found my seat and shortly after, Asia came into class, making a beeline straight to hers. I glanced at her a bit confused as to why she didn't try to show me up right then. Did she forget what she said? I brushed her off thinking maybe she decided not to take me on because she knew she would lose.

Class started and when Mr. Webster would ask questions, Asia's hand would shoot up like she just *had* to answer, except when she did, she gave off-the-wall answers and looked really dumb. Asia threw everyone off because none of us had never heard her sound so stupid. She spent the entire class acting ridiculous and when the bell rang for another class change, she rushed to Eric's desk.

"I need extra help with this class. Do you think that you can help me during lunch?" she asked. *She's clever.* I took a little longer gathering my things so that I could hear his response. I had hoped he didn't fall for it like everyone else did.

Eric looked at her. "Asia, I don't know what got into you today. You were all over the place with your answers and I know you know this material, so I am not going to entertain your behavior."

Astonished, Asia responded, "So we're not having lunch?"

"Correct," Eric replied. I took that as my cue to leave, but not before showing Asia how big of a loser she was. I had the biggest smirk on my face as I walked passed her and if looks could kill, I would have died from her gaze that day.

A couple of hours later, I was heading back to Eric's class when I heard people whispering as I walked by them. I just knew Asia told them something about me, I just didn't know what that something was.

I pranced in the class like I was going to claim my prize and as far as I was concerned, I *did* win. Eric and I began talking about my weekend and caused me to pause mid-conversation.

"You look so good today," he complimented. I wanted to say *yeah I know*, but I didn't because I was modest, so I replied with a simple thank you. He reached over to touch the necklace on my neck but then slid his hand down towards my breast.

My heart started beating fast so I closed my eyes to brace myself and wham! He kissed me and he had the softest lips I had ever felt. My emotions were popping all over the place like fireworks on the Fourth of July. At this point I really thought that I was someone special to him and that he was in love with me. Things immediately got serious. I started doodling his last name to my first name, dreaming about how our life would be together, how many kids we would have and what their names would be.

A few days later as luck would have it, Asia saw Eric at the mall with a woman, so of course she couldn't wait to throw it up in my face. She saw me go into Two J's store which I did pretty much every morning, but this morning she waited for me to come out. I barely had one foot out the door before she started with me.

"So guess who I seen at the mall yesterday?" she poked fun. I shrugged. "I seen Mr. Webster and his girlfriend!" she laughed. I kept walking as rage burned inside me, but Asia was like a leech that just wouldn't go away. She must've repeated herself a hundred times until I finally had had enough.

"Who gives a f**k!" I shouted.

Taken back and a bit amused by my anger, she responded, "Oh don't act like you don't care hoe!"

That was it. I dropped my book bag and put up my fists. My book bag must of had nosey neighbor magnets in it because people came from out of nowhere. They were chanting *"Fight! Fight! Fight!"* I wasted no time and I went in swinging.

Once again, I found myself sitting in the principal's office. Mrs. Brown asked what was going on with us two. I stared at the ceiling and didn't say a word and Asia didn't say anything either.

"Somebody better start talking and I do mean right now!" Mrs. Brown demanded. I finally blurted out "Asia was waiting for me outside of Two J's to tease me!!"

"Ok," Mrs. Brown said. "And what was she saying?" Suddenly, I got amnesia.

"uhm uhm uhm...she was just in my face." Mrs. Brown could tell by my face that I was hiding something, so she turned her attention to Asia.

"Asia, what were you saying?"

Asia glanced over at me and said, "Nothing, I was just following Monique and she snapped." I stood up aggravated and ready to throw hands again.

"Asia you weren't saying nothing! I didn't know that nothing sounded like words!" We bickered back and forth for a few moments before Mrs. Brown, who was tired of the lies, contained us both. She put her foot down and our meeting ended with yet another suspension.

Later that evening when my mom got home from work and found out that I was suspended, she called me in my room and locked the door.

"Take your clothes off" she commanded. I knew I was in trouble because she was biting her bottom lip. "Hurry up!" she yelled as she gripped a long, black belt ready to tear me up. I was running around the room trying to avoid the belt when I ran right smack into the corner of the dresser, hitting my eye and causing an instant headache.

"Stop! Stop, my eye!" I cried. Despite my pleas, she hit me a few more times before having mercy.

I needed ice or something to ease the searing pain, so I dragged myself to the kitchen. I wrapped a whole tray of ice cubes in paper towels and went to the bathroom. I stayed in the bathroom and locked the door for about 45 minutes.

"Get out that d*mn bathroom! You're not the only one that has to use it," mom yelled from the other side. My body couldn't handle feeling mom's wrath again, so I slowly opened the door and went to my room. Many thoughts danced around in my head, but it was hard to concentrate on one considering my body was screaming out in pain. I laid down, hoping that some rest would do me some good.

The next morning, she woke me up and told me that she wanted the entire house clean before she got back home since I couldn't go to school. I could hardly move or see. I had only hit one eye, but having the other one open caused even more strain. I tried my best to clean as much as I could in the condition I was in, but I just couldn't manage to have everything clean enough to meet her expectations. She came home with fire in her eyes. She looked around, got on her hands and knees and ran her finger against the floor board.

"What is this? What the hell is this? Is this dirt?" she screamed. I didn't say a word and she went to her room and flew back out swinging the cord from an iron.

"I'm so sick of you", she yelled repeatedly.

I had no energy to run so I crawled up into a ball while she whipped me senselessly. Thankfully, my stepdad came in and ordered her to stop. When she was finished, I looked like I had been a part of the movie *Roots*.

I was embarrassed to go back to school because I had so many welts. I searched for a long sleeve turtle neck to wear which was buried in my drawer. For anyone that had known me, that was a dead giveaway that something was wrong because I hated wearing things around my neck. It was a reminder of Jason putting his hand on my neck as he used his other hand to cover my mouth.

Anyway, when I got to school a few people asked me who was I in a fight with and others claimed that my eye was still bruised from my fight with Asia. I shot that rumor down quick because Asia hardly got in a hit, but a light bulb went off in my head for another reason: I finally had proof that I was being abused. I had told Mrs. Brown before that my mom was abusing me and she thought I was lying. I went in her office and asked to speak with her, but I didn't get the chance and was sent back to homeroom. After the morning announcements, I went to Ms. Garfield and whispered, "I need to go to the nurse."

"Are you sick?" she asked.

"No I need some ice for my stomach." She looked at me with unimpressed eyes and called me out into the hall.

"What kind of games are you playing young lady?"

"I'm not playing any games," I insisted as I lifted up my shirt half way. She jumped back and managed to muffle her gasps.

"Oh my gosh! Wait right here," she urged as she ran back into the class. She came back out with a hall pass and ordered me to go to the nurse and tell her exactly what happened to me. When I got to the nurse's office, I could tell she was a bit annoyed with me.

"If you were sick why did you even come to school?" she mumbled. I didn't say a word. I just lifted up my shirt and her eyes widened.

"My lord!" she exclaimed. She picked up the phone and the next thing I knew, Mrs. Brown was walking into the nurse's office.

"Follow me," the nurse said. I followed her and we went behind a curtain. "Show Mrs. Brown." I took a deep breath and showed her. Mrs. Brown hugged me.

"Child I am sorry! Come to my office," she commanded and I did. I ended up waiting there for a long time, so I asked why I was sitting there. Mrs. Brown informed me that a social worker from Children's and Youth Services was coming to talk with me. It wasn't long after that that a short, black woman came in. She introduced herself and said that she had come to offer me guidance and protection, but in order for her to do so I had to cooperate with her.

"Did someone hurt you?"

"Who was it?"

"Can I see what she did?"

"What did your mother used to cause these welts?"

"Is this the first time?"

The questions were never ending, but I answered all of them. She took some pictures of my bruises and said that as soon as she had the pictures developed she was going to come to my house for a visit. My eyes got wide and I became panicked. No one said anything about coming to my house!

CHAPTER SEVEN

The doorbell rang and it was the social worker along with a police officer. They asked to talk with my mom and stepdad first. My sister and I excused ourselves to the bedroom. Once we entered the room, I pressed my ears to the door trying my best to eavesdrop. It was hard to hear what was going on considering we were down the hall from the living room but at times I could hear my mom say "what" or "oh no"! Soon enough, I was called back to the living room. I slowly strolled into the living room and was immediately drawn to my mom because I could almost see steam coming from her ears. I glanced over at my stepdad, who looked concerned, and I knew that I was in for it.

The social worker said, "We are here talking to your parents about the bruises you had and they are unaware of the bruises that I'm speaking of." My stepfather excused himself from the room, claiming that he was going to check on my sister, but he never came back.

"I have some questions that I'm going ask you, Monique, and I would like for you to answer them truthfully", said the social worker. In my mind, I thought to plead the fifth, but then the social worker pulled out the pictures that she had taken of me and started showing them to my mom. Mom was mortified.

She then handed them to me asking, "Is this you in this pictures?" Reluctantly, I answered yes.

"Ok, so who did this to you?" I closed my eyes and took a long, deep breath. "Go ahead. it's alright," the social worker encouraged. Before I answered, I glanced at the police officer for reassurance he nodded.

"It was my mom."

"Thank you very much Monique. Now if you will excuse yourself, I need to talk with your mother for a few minutes," she said. I didn't waste any time; I rushed back to my room with the quickness. I sat on the corner of my bed against the wall holding on to my pillow not knowing what to expect next. I found myself praying to the Lord asking Him to protect me throughout the night. I listened as attentively as I could, and as soon as I heard the front door shut, I knew that the social worker and the police officer were gone and that I was in trouble. I quickly snuggled under the covers and pretended to be asleep. My mom did come to my room but she said nothing, so I guess my prayer had worked.

Just as I thought the coast was clear, in came my sister. She climbed up on my bed and pulled the covers back.

"Hey, are you sleep?" she asked. I didn't answer. "Dad said that he was so sorry for what mom did to you and he wish that he could have stopped it. I'm sorry too Monique, and I love you," 'Queena said before getting in her own bed. All the while, I just listened as I tried to fight back the tears. At least I knew *someone* loved me.

"Get up," a voice demanded – a voice I knew all too well, but her tone was of a different wavelength. I turned over and there was mom, standing over me with rage in her eyes. "The next time you call yourself reporting me, you might want to have somewhere else to go first 'cause next time I just might kill you." She left me on that note and I was terrified. I just *had* to figure out how to save myself.

I went to school and tried to have a normal day but I just couldn't stay focused. I went from class to class walking like a spaced-out zombie. My friends were talking to me and I could hear them, but I couldn't make out what they were saying. Instead, all I could do was rehearse how things were going to pan out for me once I got home and the possibilities petrified me.

It finally dawned on me that I needed to protect myself at all costs, so when I went home, I started looking for knives that my mom wouldn't necessarily miss. I swiped three knives from the knife block; I put one in a plastic ziplock bag and taped it inside of the toilet bowl, another in the living room on the side of the sofa cushions arm, and the third under my pillow. Phase one was complete, but I had to have an exit plan. I packed a small bag with a few pieces of clothes, change from my piggy bank, and a jar of applesauce just in case I needed to run away quickly and *this* time, I would be more prepared. In reality, I wouldn't have gotten far or lasted long, but there wasn't exactly an abundance of time or resources.

The time came when everyone started coming home and I felt ready to defend myself. I had everything in place and was ready to react at any given notice. Surprisingly enough, nothing happened. As a matter of fact, a couple of weeks went by and I didn't get into any trouble and trouble stayed away from me. I was able to take a deep breath and had hoped that everything was behind us and we would start fresh.

Well, that deep breath was all I could do. The social worker paid us a surprise visit and she brought more questions and concerns with her. I had to show her my body again so she would see that there were no more bruises and she then talked with my mom, which seemed to go okay. It might have been protocol, but she even asked to talk with my little sister, and boy, did that set my mom off.

"Excuse my French, but what in hell do you need to talk to her about? 'Queena had nothing to do with this situation," my mom asserted. The social worker was clearly used to that kind of reaction because she was still calm and collected.

"It's my duty to talk with and check every child that is under the age of 18 years old living in the household." Of course mom didn't like it, but she knew in order to make this go away, she had to let them talk. After speaking with my sister, the social worker asked to speak to me again privately, so we went into the kitchen away from everyone else.

"Is everything okay?" she whispered.

I replied, "I don't know because I feel like I'm going to kill myself or my mom." With a surprised look on her face she said, "Is that so?"

I could sense that behind her shock she really didn't believe me, so I attempted to prove myself. I reached down the side of the sofa and pulled out one of the knives. I got her attention, but I still didn't think that I convinced her.

"Come follow me," I suggested, as I lead her to the bathroom and pulled the knife from the toilet bowl lid. I was then sure that she was convinced, but why stop there?

"I have one more knife in my room," I casually shared but when I went to go get it I saw that 'Queena was in the room. I didn't want her to know that I had a knife under my pillow, so I looked at the social worker and said, "Just believe me."

My little tour prompted all types of questions, but the one that I remember was, "are you planning on killing yourself or your mother tonight?"

"I'm not going to kill myself tonight, but I might kill my mom if she tries to beat me", I replied.

The social worker was beyond disturbed, but to me, that was a good thing; it meant that she was going to help me.

"Listen," she began. "If there was anyone in the world that you could live with, who would that be?" she asked. That was the easiest question ever.

"My grandmom," I replied.

"Okay, do you think that your grandmother would like for you to live with her?" she asked.

"Yeah, my grandmom loves me!"

She smiled at me. "Ok then. I am going to work on you moving with your grandmother, but first I need for you to do me a favor. I want you to write down all the things that you love about your mother and show me tomorrow. Can you do that for me?" It was an odd request, but I agreed.

I managed to write down a few things but my list wasn't as long as I wanted it to be. I wanted to love my mom way more than what I did, but she just didn't deserve it. I think I felt that way because I didn't believe she loved me, however, it was apparent that she *cared* about me, which is different. I was treated more like a stepchild than her biological daughter. I fell asleep pondering my list and wishing all of this could go away, but before I knew it, it was morning. Around 8:30 a.m. or so, Ms. Social Worker came to my house with the police. She handed my mom some papers and said that she was there to remove me from the home.

"After speaking with Monique last night, I have determined that she needs psychological help because of homicidal and suicidal thoughts. It is what's best for everyone." There was only a short pause in the air before mom interrupted the awkward moment.

"What in the world are you talking about?"

"Well," said the social worker, "Monique had hidden knives around the house because she was afraid of you hurting her. She had plans to hurt you or herself." That was only half true because yes I had plans on hurting her, but it was predicated on her hurting me. Self-defense, you see?

"Please go and pack a bag Monique, we have to go." I ran in the bedroom so quick and threw more of my clothes in the bag than I had already packed. Returning to the living room less than two minutes later, the social worker complimented my swiftness while my mom stood there speechless as if she couldn't comprehend what was going on.

I was raring to go; I was so excited, I left the house without even saying goodbye. The officer opened the back door of a dark blue car, I hopped in, and off we went.

As giddy as I was to finally be out of that house on my way to grandmom's, my mood slowly began to change when I noticed that the social worker was not going to my grandmother's house, at least not the way that I was used to going, but I just laid back and thought she knew a different way.

Boy, was I wrong.

CHAPTER EIGHT

"Come on," said the social worker. "You need to get out." We arrived at this big, spooky gray building and I didn't understand why I needed to get out; my grandmother didn't live there, so I wasn't moving. I shook my head no. I glanced around, hoping to find some type of indication of where I was and why.

"Philadelphia Psychiatric Center" the sign on the building read as it illuminated the street. At that moment, I couldn't figure out why we were there, but I was soon going to find out. We walked in the building and were instantly greeted with strange people. I was scared to even flinch around some of them because there was no telling what they would do.

"I'm here to check Monique Fisher in," Ms. Social Worker said once we got to the front desk.

"Say what?! Check me in? For what?!" I asked.

"Sweetie, there are some people here that will take good care of you," she responded.

"But-but-but where is my grandmom?" I stuttered. I looked around franticly, desperately looking for an escape.

"She will be notified that you are here and she will come get you when the program is over." I felt the room freeze and the words she spoke replayed in my head. What in the world did I get myself into? I had no business being there; I mean, I was just acting crazy but these people were *really* crazy and looked like it too. The male orderly took my bags as a lady lead me to my room. As we trekked on through the hallways, I began to feel a little more at ease, as everything started looking a little better.

"We're here," the lady said opening the door. As the orderly placed my bags on the floor, he winked at me before walking out and closing the door behind him. My gaze trailed him as he left my sight and all the while, I couldn't figure out if I should have been weirded out or flattered.

"By the way, my name is Marbella, but people call me Bella. I need for you to change into these clothes and while you are doing that, can you please open your bags?" I opened them without a fuss, though there wasn't much to see in there. As I was putting on the ugly two-piece sage green uniform, she began going through my things.

"I'm going to put your bags in lock up and I will be back in a few to check on you, so get yourself settled."

"Excuse me, why are you taking my bags?" I asked. I wanted to yank them out of her hand, but the vibe this place gave me was saying I wouldn't be very successful – they'd have me locked down in a minute.

"You have everything that you need here, so you have no need for these things," Bella explained. Two knocks on the door and the orderly reentered the room to take my bags.

The room was depressing; it was more of a cell than a room and the beds were more like cots. The mattress was so thin I could fold it in half. Seriously - a waffle was thicker than it was. As I started making up my bed, in came this super tall and skinny girl with long blonde spiked hair.

"Hi," she greeted. "I'm Sara. I guess you're my new roommate?" I nodded my head but didn't say a thing. "Okay cool. I was getting bored talking to myself."

I didn't stand a chance. She must've been waiting for a long time to have someone to chat with because she started talking as if it was going out of style. She went on and on and on and before I could completely answer one question, she was on to the next.

I was ever so glad when Bella knocked on the door. *Oh thank heavens!* I thought to myself. She could not have come at a better time and I was beyond sick and tired of Sara talking my ear off. Bella took me on a tour of the facilities and she also gave me a schedule of when different activities took place. For breakfast, lunch, and dinner I was expected to attend on my own; If I didn't show up, I didn't eat. I also couldn't miss classes - if I didn't show up, I would be placed in isolation.

Several days went by since I got there and I noticed that other patients had visitors, but no one had come to visit me. Why hadn't anyone come for me or visited me yet? Why didn't my mother come for me? Why didn't she try to get me out of there? I know that I had been a troublesome child, but I was still her daughter. I was starting to think she never really wanted me, and it took being sent to a nuthouse to come to terms with that. With a heavy, broken heart, I shuffled to the help desk to inquire as to when my grandmother would be picking me up.

"Your name again?" the lady asked while glancing down at a big gray book. After giving her my name, she assured me that I had a scheduled visit coming up in two days, however, it didn't say with who. Sara later told me that you had to be a residence of P.P.C. for a full week before visitors could come to visit and that there were only two visiting days per week, so that made me feel a little better.

Those next two days were two of the longest days ever, but I got through them and I was itching to see some familiar faces with the hopes that they would take me away with them. When I went to the visiting area, I didn't see anyone that I recognized, so I sat down, grabbed a magazine, and made myself comfortable. I hadn't quite settled in yet before Ms. Social Worker sat in front of me.

"Why are *you* here?" I asked. I looked around hoping that someone else was with her, someone I *actually* wanted to see.

"I'm here to check on you and to see how you are adjusting." I just looked at her with a blank stare on my face. "So how are you?" she asked.

"Where's my grandmom?" I replied. She then looked at me with a similar blank stare I was giving her. "Well?"

She sighed. "Your grandmother will be here to visit you real soon, but besides that, how are you doing?" Since I got my answer, I was ready to get out of there, but before I made my exit, I had a bone to pick with her.

"I'm ok, but why did you lie to me?" I probed. "You said that I could go live with my grandmother and you brought me here."

"No dear, I didn't lie to you. There is a process that we have to go through before that can happen. There are some legal matters that have to be handled and you, my dear, have to be released from this program," she explained. Did she really think that I cared about legal stuff? All I cared about was being with my grandmom. I thought for a second.

"So what do I have to do to get out of here?"

"Simple," she began. "Follow instructions, go to your classes, go to your evaluation sessions, and stay out of trouble." I nodded while thinking, *Okay I could do that...let the games begin!*

From that day forward, I was going to be the first one in class, arrive to my evaluation sessions early, and I was going to be the sweetest, friendliest person there. A few weeks went by, and everyone was impressed with how pleasant I was. I made so many friends, everyone knew who I was, and everyone wanted to be around me. Even Bella pulled me to the side and told me how much my teachers were impressed with how well I was doing in their classes and how my evaluator gave me good reviews. Every day I spent acting right, was another day closer to leaving with my grandmom, so I intended to stay on that path towards freedom.

But of course, nothing lasts forever right? I should have known my patience was going to get tested, but I just couldn't see too far ahead of me to see that one mistake could set me back so much.

One morning at breakfast, the cafeteria lady began putting mush resembling dog food on my tray, though as disgusted as I was, I sweetly said, "no, no thank you!"

"It's good, you should try it. It's corn beef hash," she explained. I had never heard of nor had I ever seen corn beef hash before, but I was willing to taste it, so I took it. I found a place to sit, but before I could sit down, this girl who I never saw before said to me, "don't sit there that's my seat." I looked at her and sat down anyway.

"Didn't I just tell you not to sit in my seat?" she said getting in my face.

"I'm sorry, I didn't see your name on this seat," I responded. So I started to eat and just as I tasted the corn beef hash, she said,

"Oh, I see you are a b*tch 'cause only dogs eat that sh*t." I ignored her, and was doing so well too - until she flipped my tray over. Oh, she struck a chord. I rose from my seat, picked the tray up, and smacked her with it. She went tumbling to the ground, cupping her head, and to add insult to injury, I took what was left of the corn beef and smashed it in her face.

"Who's eating sh*t now?!"

Orderlies came running, pushing through the crowd toward us shouting, "Break it up!", as if it was a fight. It wasn't a fight; I was standing and she was on the floor holding her head. One of the orderlies grabbed me and escorted me to a small room.

"Why am I here?"

"You were fighting and this is where we have to bring y'all when y'all decide to be violent," he clarified before shutting the door and leaving. I had heard of The Hole from Sara, but she never really described it to me. The Hole was a pint sized room - no bigger than a bathroom stall - without a toilet or any windows. There was no furniture in the room and lights were very dim.

I sat on the floor and couldn't help but cry because I didn't deserve to be in there and I was scared. There was no clock in the room, so the only way I knew the time was by the meals that I was served. At lunch time, they opened up the slot in the door and passed me my food. I was so upset that I couldn't even eat. The food sat in front of me for hours before I started pretending like the food was people. I had made a whole community out of my lunch. As I was in deep conversation with the french-fries, my therapist came in. I froze up just like a popsicle and stared at my edible mini-town, embarrassed.

"Who were you talking to?" she asked. I took a minute before answering to weigh my options. If I told her that I was talking to my food, she would definitely think I was crazy so I said I had to think of something else.

"No one. I was singing to myself," I knew it was a lie, but so did she because what I hadn't realized was that she was at the door listening to play with my food. So after asking me what had happened that landed me in the hole, she gave me a disappointed, "and you were doing so good". The door shut and I was all alone again.

Dinner time came, and the orderly opened the slot on the door and told me to slide my lunch tray to him and then he would slide me my dinner. This was my chance – I had to get out of that room – even if it meant just to take a breath.

I yelled, "Hey, I have to go to the bathroom!" A few seconds later, the door opened and another orderly escorted me to the bathroom. I actually did have to use it, but it was nice to be on the outside of that room for a bit.

"How am I supposed to let y'all know when I have to go again because I was holding myself for a long time," I inquired as we headed back to The Hole. The orderly didn't say a word but when we got back to the Hole he stepped in and pointed to a button on the wall

"You push this button when you need to go," and off he went. Had I done something so wrong that I needed to be placed in such a place? Did I kill the girl? She was alive when the orderlies took me away. What could I have possible done that was so terrible? I was defending myself. Where was the girl at? Was she in a hole too?

My stomach grumbled so I decided to eat a little something since I didn't know how long it would be before I got something else to eat. With every bite, I began to get really sick and it wasn't long before that feeling came over me and my mouth filled with the slop that I was fed all day. I released it and though I felt a tad bit better, I still couldn't shake the uneasy feeling. I wasn't crazy, but being in the hole started making feel like I was.

When I woke up the next morning, the room reeked. I hit the button for the bathroom break, and soon enough another orderly opened the door and was greeted by the stench and immediately backed away.

"What is that smell?" he asked.

"Oh I throw up," I said.

"We'll clean it up," he insisted while holding his nose.

"Do you know why am I in here? 'Cause all I did was defend myself," I maintained. He said that he didn't know because he wasn't on duty yesterday but if I was nice to him he would find out. After cleaning my hole, he said that he would be back, and not too long after that, he was and this time, with some answers.

"So, they told me that you were placed in here because you threatened the cafeteria lady by telling her that you would make her eat sh*t if she kept trying to make you eat sh*t. They also said you said you would break her legs and make her crawl around like a dog to eat," he explained. I could tell he was even somewhat entertained by that complete lie that had just come out of his mouth.

"I didn't say anything like that at all! I asked her what it was that she was placing on my tray and after she told me I tried eating it and liked the corn beef hash." I explained. "Can you please ask her if I was the one who said that to her?" I pleaded.

He smirked. "I can do that, but what will you do for me?" he asked.

"What do you want me to do?"

"Well if you take care of me, I'll take care of you."

"Uhm okay," I agreed. I thought it was a reasonable deal. He would look out for me and I would look out for him even though I wasn't sure how I would do that. He left me alone once again and came back with my breakfast, but this time he brought the food in the room instead of passing it to me through the door.

"Here's the deal. You can come out of The Hole after breakfast but you have to do a few things for me."

"Ok, what?" I asked.

"One, I need this arrangement to stay between us, and two, I want you to make me cum whenever I ask you to. Agreed?" he requested.

"Sure, it's a deal!" I exclaimed with glee. He had a strange way of communicating because this wasn't the first time that I really didn't know what he meant, but who cared? I was going to get out of The Hole.

"Hit the button once you are done eating and I'll be back to get you," he said.

"Wait, wait!" I yelled to stop him. "Since we are going to be good buddies, don't you think that I should know your name?" I insisted.

"Of course. It's Tony," he responded with a smirk. He left me again, and I ate that breakfast so quick, I was hitting the button in less than three minutes. When Tony came in the room he laughed and suggested that I must have been hungry because I had eaten in record time.

"Ok, let me see if you have what it takes. Man, you are so pretty and your body is like a goddess," he admired as he inched closer to me. *Here he goes again,* I thought. I had no idea what a goddess was or what one would look like. He told me to turn against the wall and when I did, his hands began roaming my body. As he grabbed my breast, he rubbed up against me and I felt him get hard. Tears filled my eyes but I knew not to move. He dropped his pants and started rubbing his penis on my butt.

"You are making me feel so good," he whispered to me, sending shivers throughout my body. He started to moan and groan as he rubbed harder and quicker against me. The next thing I knew he had white stuff coming out of him and he released it into the bucket that he had left there from earlier.

"You did it! I knew you could make me cum," he applauded. *Oh no,* I thought. *That's what he was talking about!* I felt ashamed and horrible because I agreed to make him cum whenever he wanted to. I got myself together, trying to pretend like nothing happened.

"Can I go now?" I quickly asked, wiping away the last traces of tears. He opened the door and I ran out. I went to my room got some clothes and went to the shower room to wash. I was shaking so badly, I could hardly wash up. I got dressed, went back to my room and huddled in the corner. I hated the fact that men thought that they could violate me with no regard of my feelings. I was only a child. The only thing running through my mind was, maybe I *should* kill myself.

About two weeks later, I just wasn't feeling good so I told Sara that I was going to stay in the room and I asked her to bring me something to eat like a muffin or Danish since it was against the rules to bring food to the rooms. I was sure that she could manage to sneak that in the room without getting caught, but she was way too obvious and talked way too much. Of all people to catch her in the act, Tony had stopped her and asked her where was she going with the food that he saw her put under her shirt. She blabbed and explained to him that she was bringing it to the room for me because I was sick.

Apparently, Tony told her that he would bring me a meal and for her not to worry about it. I almost fell off the bed when he walked in the room.

"You're sick?" he asked.

"Um yeah I don't feel well," I answered.

"Sara told me that you were hungry so I brought you something to eat and I bet that I can make you feel better!" he claimed. "Here, lie down and relax," Tony told me as he started to rub my head. It only took him a few moments to direct his attention somewhere else; he started rubbing my breasts and complimented me on how firm they were.

"Does it feel good?" he asked me. I lied and said yes because I was scared to say anything else. He lifted his hand off of me as if he had just been electrocuted or something – as if he now harbored some sort of energy from touching me. He swore he would be right back and left the room. I was frozen and still feeling too bad to get up and make any kind of run for it. A minute or so later, he came back with a chair and he placed the chair under the door handle and proceeded to finish what he started. He pulled down his pants and moved me over to lay in the bed with me, pulling my pants down too after he got us both situated.

"Have you ever ridden a horse?" he asked. I shook my head.

"I'm going to show you how. Get on top on me," instructed Tony.

"I don't want to learn how to ride a horse," I cried. I did my best to stall, but it wasn't working at all.

"Oh come on, it will be fun and plus you made me a promise." I flashed back to me eagerly agreeing to make him happy whenever he wanted to and hated myself for being so naive. "Sit on my dick."

I glanced down at it and almost immediately blurted out, "How it's sticking up?" He chuckled and said "just sit on it." When I sat on it, he instructed me on what to do.

"That's it. Faster... faster...." he moaned. The faster I went, the more tired I got and I eventually had to stop, though he begged me not to. I guess Tony could tell that I was tired because he placed me on the bed and pulling my underwear off while he rubbed up against me.

"Oh my god, oh my god, oh my god!" he panted as the white stuff squirted all over my stomach. He bent down and kissed my vagina to show his appreciation.

"You are so good to me, and one day I'm going to come inside."

I laid there as he collected himself and left. As soon as the door shut, I proceeded to clean myself off. As I freshened up, I started to think about how I could get out of P.P.C.; There were bars on every window, wired fences and guards, and even if I did make it to the outside courtyard, the exit to the sidewalk was like five miles away. I had to find somewhere to hide because Tony could come to my room for me at any time. I jumped up and went on a search for a safe place for me to hide out.

It was not easy but after a fairly short search, I found my safe haven. In the library, there was a display table that had a long tablecloth on it, so I decided to grab a few books and when no one was looking, I crawled under.

Soon, I realized that it was lunch time and I had to eat. I had to wait a long time before I felt it was safe for me to crawl out. At lunch, some of my friends were asking what happened because they heard that I was sent to The Hole. One of my friends, Jill, explained that the girl that I had got into a fight with was new and that the orderlies thought that the cafeteria lady was talking about me when really she was talking about the new girl. The new girl heard that I was popular and she wanted that title, so she thought that she could bully me out of it.

"Are ya'll willing to tell my therapist that story so that she would know that I wasn't lying," I asked. Only two agreed so I, along with the two friends, went to Mrs. Jones office and they told her what happened. It was clear Mrs. Jones doubted us, but she promised she would verify our story with the cafeteria lady. Not only did the cafeteria lady confirm my story, but Mrs. Jones apologized to me for not believing me when I first told her what happened. The icing on the cake was the vow made to believe me, but despite being tempted to tell her what Tony did to me, I still was hesitant to let that secret out; after not being believed so many times, it was just hard to trust that people were going to take me seriously, even if they said they would.

For several days, I managed to avoid Tony, not realizing that I was also hiding from everyone else too. My friends started saying how they haven't seen me around other than class and meal times. Rumor had it that I was staying away from Joelinda, but the problem with that was, I didn't even know who that was. I asked Sara, who seemed to be in the know about everything around P.P.C.

"She's the girl that you knocked out. I've been trying to tell you that that's what being going around but you always seem to be sleep." I wasn't always asleep - I was ignoring her because she talked so much about every and anything and it all ran together so it just never made sense to me.

"What kind of name is Joelinda? No wonder why she's angry. I would be too with a crazy name like that," I joked. "I'm not afraid of nobody, so she can take that lie and bury it 'cause it's dead!" I exclaimed. I had to set the record straight.

"So where have you been, and why aren't you at any of our activities?" Jill asked me.

"Will y'all stop with the questions?" I huffed. "I've been in the library, okay?" Disbelief and mockery washed across their faces so I did a little explaining, which eventually led me to showing them. I presented my table to them and they gave me the most bewildered look.

I looked them all in the eyes and said, "What I'm about to tell you, none of you can repeat. If you do, I will kill you and I'm not playing." I took a deep breath. "I've been hiding out here under the table because Tony likes me and I don't like him."

"Tony likes everybody," Keara interjected.

"No he *really* likes me. He touches me and he hurt me," I explained. It felt so good to finally release that secret, but when I looked at their widened eyes and mouths wide open, I could tell that I wasn't the only one with that burden.

"Me too. He hurt me too," Vette said. I certainly wasn't expecting to tell anyone what was happening, but I most definitely wasn't ready to hear that it was happening to one of my own friends too. I embraced Vette and we sobbed and as we released, I could feel the load lighten from both her and I. Keara and Sara both agreed that we should snitch on Tony because if he was doing it to us, there was no telling who else he was doing things to.

"Go to Mrs. Jones! I think she would believe you," Jill insisted. Vette and I glanced at each other and agreed to do it together. There was power in numbers, and with our friends behind us, we were sure to get Tony to stop, or better – fired and put in jail. Mrs. Jones was usually always in her office, so when we went there and she wasn't, we couldn't help but think that maybe it was a sign that it wasn't a good idea to tell her. I wouldn't say we gave up hope, but our eagerness certainly went down. We proceeded to go about our day, but just as we turned the corner we eyeballed Mrs. Jones coming right towards us.

"Hi girls! I was just looking for you, Monique," she greeted. "I have good news for you. Come with me," she instructed. She started towards her office, and Yvette and I trotted after her.

"Vette and I were just coming from your office to talk to you, so can she come too?" I inquired.

"Yes, sure. We'll talk first and then we will call her in," Mrs. Jones affirmed. I gave Vette a reassuring smile and when we got back to her office, I went in first.

"Great news! Your paper work has been finalized and you are eligible for an earlier release. Your grandmother will be here in a few days to pick you up!" she said happily. I dropped my head because if I didn't do anything to stop Tony he would still hurt Vette. "What's wrong? I thought that you would be thrilled to hear that," probed Mrs. Jones.

"I am excited, but Vette and I have to tell you something and I don't think that you will be as happy as you are right now," I insinuated. With a worried look, Mrs. Jones called Vette in the office.

"Alright ladies what's going on?"

"Mrs. Jones do you remember when you told me that the next time I tell you something that you would believe me?" I asked. She reluctantly affirmed.

"I was telling my friends the reason why they didn't see me much anymore and Vette told me that it happened to her too by Tony."

"I'm not sure what you are trying to say," she said scratching her head.

Vette interjected. "Tony touches me and Monique and we don't like it." Mrs. Jones slowly sat down in her chair and put her hand on her head.

"Tony touched you both in your private areas?" she whispered. Simultaneously we both said yes. We learned a lot that day; apparently, we weren't the first ones she heard that from. There was another girl a while ago who told her teacher the same thing, but no one believed her. She tied one end of her bed sheet to a staircase and the other around her neck and jumped, killing herself. I heard the story before, but it was way before my time there and since there was no name attached to the story, I kind of thought it was made up.

"Are y'all willing to say this in front of him along with other adult staff?" Mrs. Jones inquired.

Vette shouted, "Hell no! What if they don't believe us and he continues to work here and he hurts us? No, I'm not doing it!" Since I was leaving in a few days, I had nothing to lose, but I couldn't leave Yvette there without any hope, so I came up with an idea.

"Mrs. Jones I want to be put in The Hole." I said.

"I don't understand," Mrs. Jones stated.

"If I am put in The Hole and Tony knows that I'm in there, he will come in there and touch me. So, someone can watch him and see when he comes. If y'all wait about five minutes and walk in, I bet y'all would catch him," I plotted. It was a pretty good plan for me having just thought of it, if I did say so myself.

"Why would you be willing to go through that?" asked Mrs. Jones.

"One, so that you will believe us and two, because I don't want to leave my friends here with someone that will hurt them," I answered.

"You're leaving?" Vette asked.

"Yes. That was the good news that she wanted to tell me." Mrs. Jones sat quietly and I could tell by the look on her face, she was thinking deeply.

"One minute." She called in her boss and another co-worker to run the situation by them and once everyone agreed, I was put in The Hole that night.

Just as I predicted, Tony came in the room but for some reason he wanted to take his time getting started. I knew that we didn't have a whole lot of time, so I started to tell him how much

I missed him and how I liked making him happy blah, blah, blah and he was pretty quick to drop his pants.

"I wanted to do something special since I'm going to be leaving in a few days," I told him. "I want to give you something to remember me by." He halted his typical eye seduction he did when he was ready to take advantage of me.

"Wait you're leaving in a few days? Then why are you in The Hole?" he asked. Well, *that* was a good question.

Thinking quickly, I said, "Well, this was the only way that I could think of for us to be together before leaving." He cackled

"You're crazy. You're not going anywhere for a while. Once you are put in here, it adds more time to your stay." He continued to laugh, but the joke was really on him because I had already been processed out and he was about to be found out.

"Oh well! I guess I have longer to make you feel good then," I flirted.

That did it - I made him so hot, that he practically ripped off all his clothes. Before he could even touch me, the door opened and he almost had a heart attack. Of course, I pretended to have one too because I didn't want him to know that I was the brains behind the whole operation. In short, Tony was caught and fired, my friends were now safe, and I was being discharged from P.P.C.

CHAPTER NINE

"Grandmom, Grandmom!" I yelled as I leaped into her arms. It seemed like forever since the last time I saw her and life at that moment couldn't get any better. I jumped in the car and fastened my seatbelt with the biggest smile on my face, but as we pulled off, tears begin to seamlessly stream. What I wouldn't have done to have that feeling of happiness and love last forever. I couldn't help but think about what Jason and Tony had done to me and how much happiness they had taken from me. I wanted to tell my grandmother about Tony but I just couldn't bring myself to hurt her.

I closed my eyes as tight as I could. *Everything is going to be alright, so smile*, I thought to myself. *No one will ever hurt you again.* An hour or so later, we pulled up to my grandmother's house. It was a duplex, so I actually moved in with my aunt Juanita – Nita for short - who lived upstairs, while my grandmother was living downstairs with her boyfriend, Reggie. It was kind of cool, but my aunt was an early bird so I was bored a lot of the time; there was no cable TV or anything else for me to do other than play Solitaire on the computer.

A month or so later, I was able to get back in touch with Trina and we talked here and there. I told her about all the crazy mess I'd been through and she told me about her mother's drug habit and how it got worse, so she had to move in with her uncle. We were two troubled kids with two different backstories, but I was glad to know that no matter what happened to me in life, I could always tell Trina about it. I told her that I was a little nervous, because soon I would be going back to Pulaski, where I had gotten into so much trouble before. She assured me that things may be different and that I shouldn't worry. Plus, I had her, so in the very least, I was going back to school with one friend.

My aunt drove me to school since the school was across town. I still managed to worry about some of the bridges that may have been burned, but when I got there, I was relieved to be able to start fresh. I had no problems with anyone and only some of the people I knew were there from before while others were long gone including Eric and Mrs. Brown. Everything else was as I remembered and it was as if I never left.

One day, my aunt Nita asked her boyfriend, Jeff, to take me to school since he had stayed over and she was running late for work. He had a flashy bright red sports car, so I definitely didn't have a problem with him taking me. He was really cool and nice. He asked me if I had money for lunch, and even when I said yes, he still gave me extra money for snacks.

It soon became normal for him to take me to school - even when he didn't stay the night, he would still come and get me, not that I minded; I was being dropped off in a cool car and he was giving me money. One morning, I forgot my lunch, but didn't make a big deal of it because I knew Jeff would give me some money. Before pulling up to the school I asked him if he could drop me off in front of Two J's sandwich shop.

"Why you need to go there?" He asked a bit puzzled.

"I left my lunch at home so I want to get a sandwich for school." He said okay and pulled up to the sandwich shop without any fuss. As he reached into his pocket to give me some money, he winced, pulling his hand back out.

"Ouch! I hit my hand this morning and its really sore. Can you get the money out of my pocket?" he asked. I reached over, put my hand in his pocket and I didn't feel anything. There was no money in his pocket, it was empty.

"Oh, it's there. You just need to go further into my pocket." *How deep were his pockets?* He took his left hand and put it in his pants as he guided my hand and said "Do you feel it yet?" I felt something, but it wasn't money, so I snatched my hands out of his pocket.

"Why did you jump? It's not going to bite you!" he laughed while reaching into his jacket pocket, bringing out a $20 bill. He never gave me that much before, but I knew it was hush money, so I took it and jumped out of the car. It seemed like this was the start of yet another unavoidable violation, but hey, I had $20.

The next morning's ride was so awkward. He knew that I was uncomfortable with what happened the day before. When we pulled up at my school, I jumped out not giving him a chance to say anything. I didn't even want his money. Granted, I still had money left over from the day before, but regardless, I didn't want to entertain him anymore than I had to and I was glad that I dodged that bullet. As I walked into the school, I looked back and was a little surprised he was still sitting there. I didn't know why he didn't pull off, but to be honest, I didn't care.

Weeks went by and he would pick me up and drop me off as if nothing happened, though we both knew better. He didn't say much to me other than good morning or have a good day and the money stopped coming too; he didn't offer and I didn't ask.

I thought that I had rid myself of Jeff for good when my aunt took me to school one day; I thought maybe she and Jeff broke up or something, but just my luck, he was out of town and the rides resumed once he got back. He was so bubbly and chatty.

"You haven't been talking to me. I'm guessing that I've done something to upset you, so I'm sorry."

I cut my eyes at him, but accepted his apology.

"I'm cool. Thanks for the apology," I told him.

"Good. I'm glad that we were good again," he said with a wide smile.

The very next day, he claimed that he needed to stop at his barber shop first to get something.

"Since I'm responsible for you, you needed to come in with me." I huffed at the delay he was causing me to be in, but I followed him into the shop and stayed right by the door. I glanced around the empty, dim room and a strange feeling came over me. I noticed he didn't draw back the curtains that would have invited a lot more light into the space. People would have certainly known we were in there had he opened them, so my guess was that he wanted us being there to remain a secret to the public.

"Come on," he called back to me. I didn't budge, so he came back for me, grabbed my arm, causing me to shutter. Despite my uncomfortable vibes, he continued lead me to backroom.

"Take a seat. I have a few things to take care of," he explained. All I wanted to do was get to school and away from him, but ignoring him could cause me more problems than I wanted, so I sat down. Next thing I knew, I could hear soft music playing.

"I think you were mad at me because you didn't understand what I was introducing you to," he said, inching towards me. I shook my head, hoping he would catch the hint.

"Relax, I'm going to take good care of you." He went to rub my face, and I closed my eyes, trying to figure out what I could do to get out of the situation. I guess he took that as a sign of approval. "If you like that, you're going to love this," he presumed.

"Please stop... please stop," I whispered. I guess in some sick way, it was turning him on because he didn't stop - he only continued to touch me, working his way lower and lower down my body.

"I got to go to school," I stuttered when he reached below my hips.

"I'll get you there soon." He told me to stand up and I did so, thinking *great, lets' go*, but instead, he pulled my skirt up and told me to sit back down, but this time on him.

"Touch it," he insisted as he exposed himself. I shook my head again.

"No thanks," I murmured.

"You touched it before when I was giving you all that money," he said, insinuating that I did that on purpose. "If you don't, I'm going to tell your aunt that you tried to kiss me," he said.

"But I didn't," I responded.

"Who do you think she'll believe, me or you?" he questioned. I had to take a moment to answer that myself. I couldn't be sure that she would believe me and if she did, I just know she would be so mad at me. I grabbed his jewels with so much force that he jumped and winced.

"Not that hard! Just stroke it," he said. Helpless, I complied. He then proceeded to lay the seat down, sat on top of me, and started grinding on me.

"Don't it feel good?" he asked. I didn't answer him because I didn't know how to. It felt good but I didn't want him to know it because I still wanted him to stop. He turned me over, took his penis, and rubbed it up and down my butt. With every moan he uttered, I died a little more inside.

When he was finished, he gave me a facial towel and instructed me to clean up in the bathroom. I was empty inside. *What in the world was wrong with me that these men feel the need to do this to me?*

I felt so worthless. God must have hated me or something and perhaps I wasn't meant to be born. My very existence was only so that I could be hurt, and I couldn't share my pain with anyone who could help me because who would believe me? How was I going to tell my aunt Nita that her boyfriend was a jerk? I couldn't say anything because I didn't want to hurt her, so I held on to the pain. It was only just one more secret to keep…

CHAPTER TEN

Hello God, are you there?

Do you hear me? I heard that you are real!

If you are, could you please stop my hearting from bleeding?

For a few months, I thought that God really heard my prayer and that He was really healing my heart. I was happy; I was doing well in school, I was staying out of trouble, and things were just *good*. And then... well, do you want to tell the story, because by now I'm sure you could almost do so. My life for the most part was running through the same vicious cycle - I was always someone's prey.

It is my belief that Mr. Lester over heard my grandmother or aunt talk about the things that had happened to me and that's why he had enough nerve to make his move. He called me downstairs from the hallway where the door to my aunt's apartment was. I came down and he claimed he needed my help. Something had "fallen" under his bed and he wanted to see if I could reach it because I was smaller. I had no reservations in helping since Mr. Lester was my grandmother's boyfriend and he had never given me a reason to question his behavior. He always treated me nicely from a distance – and by that, I mean that he was never up in my face and that was probably the reason for my ease when I was around him.

I bounced into the bedroom expecting to help, not knowing that I was walking into a trap. As I walked in the room, I could hear people on the television moaning. I closed eyes and turned my back to the TV.

"What do you need me to get," I asked, bending down to reach under the bed. I had to be the dumbest person alive to think that he really wanted my help.

"Oh never mind I'll get it later. Have you seen this before?" he asked referring to what was playing on the TV. I wanted to say no, but yes came out because I remembered when Lewis played a similar movie.

"You can watch it if you want to," Mr. Lester insisted.

"No, I'm good. I'll just go back upstairs and watch TV," I replied.

"I think you may want to sit and watch it with me," he asserted, but I wasn't interested in entertaining him, that dirty movie, or his dirty thoughts.

"It's okay." I put some pep in my step but before I could get out the door, he said something that made me stop in my tracks.

"Well, I wonder what your grandmother is going to think when I tell her that you were being fresh with me. She might put you back in that place she got you from." Immediately tears began to form in my eyes as several thoughts came in my mind.

She's going to believe him.

She's going to take me back.

She's not going to want me anymore.

She's going to be mad at me.

She's not going to love me anymore.

It all rushed to my mind so quickly but I maintained my composure and stood my ground.

"But I wasn't being fresh with you."

"Yes you were. I always see you walk around with those tights on and you be teasing me." Once again, I was being blamed, but I didn't understand it because I wore tights around everybody.

"I'm sorry. I didn't mean to."

"Just come here and sit."

At that point, I didn't know what other option I had. If I ran, where would I run to? How many hours would I be out waiting until my grandmother or aunt came home? I knew that I had no choice.

"If I sit down and watch it, will you tell my grandmother?" He said that he wouldn't, so I gave in. A solid minute hadn't passed yet before he put his hand on my thigh. I gulped as I began to think the worst.

"Do you have panties on?" he asked me. I nodded yes.

"Take them off. I want to smell them."

I looked at him as if he had ten heads. Why in the world would he want to smell my underwear? I had so many thoughts running through my head, but I learned not to ask to questions – they never get answered anyways.

"It's going to be okay. I promise not to hurt you," he asserted. Those words were too familiar to take him seriously, but the icing on the cake was that I witnessed him actually put my undies up to his face and inhale deeply. The very sight of it made me shiver. Through all my experiences, I had never seen anyone do something so odd and that in itself caused my nerves to quake.

"Relax," he repeated as he leaned me back on the bed. He got down on his knees and began kissing my leg. I was still quivering, so he had to hold my leg still. My breathing got heavier and heavier and my heart practically beat out of my chest as he started moved further up my leg until he reached my inner thighs.

God, what happened? What did I do? I felt like my heart was going to explode. I couldn't take it anymore; out of nowhere I screamed to the top of my lungs, releasing all the tension and nerves I was holding on to from the moments prior. I guessed I startled him because he immediately jumped up and asked if I was crying. I continued to wail until he finally gave me the space to leave.

"Go ahead, go!" he hollered. I didn't waste a second; I bolted out that room, leaving my underwear and the last straw behind.

I went upstairs and rushed straight for the knife block because I was going to kill him if he came upstairs. I sat in fear of what might happen and couldn't help but think that offing myself would better. I took the knife and proceeded to cut my wrist, but I couldn't bring myself to finish the job.

I knew that I was acting weird when my aunt came home but to avoid any questions being asked, I just told her that I wasn't feeling good and that I was going to take a bath and go to bed. I sat in the tub thinking about death. As I examined the suds surrounding me, I slowly sunk my head under the water and held my breath. After a few seconds, my lungs began to contract and I realized I was not ready for what a watery death would feel like. I spared myself the agony as I sat hopeless and desperate for a miracle.

It was so awkward seeing Lester after that, so I did my best to avoid facing him, though I couldn't escape him completely. I began having nightmares that he was going to come upstairs in the middle of the night and attack me and I was in constant torment because of it. I just wanted to die, but I could never bring myself to end it on my own.

What made this violation different then all the rest was the devastation that it could cause to the one person who had always been there for me. If she found out what happened she probably wouldn't want me anymore.

"Okay, so what's going on?" grandmother asked me one day. "You've been acting weird lately."

I hesitated to answer. "I can't tell you because you might get really mad and put me away."

"I'd never put you away," she assured me. When she caressed my cheek, I decided to take the chance in telling her. I explained everything, but when I did, her gaze was baffling to me. She wasn't angry or sad – in fact, she looked somewhat calm, which was a surprise. She didn't react, but I could tell in her eyes that she was contemplating something.

"Okay. Go upstairs." I did what she asked and left just knowing that she didn't believe a word I said.

Weeks went by and she said that we were moving to another place. Later I found out that she confronted Mr. Lester and he surprisingly admitted to everything.

"I was looking for his gun, because I was going to kill him, but the Lord didn't allow me to find it," she told me.

Once again, my grandmother proved to be my "shero". Even though I was not happy that she had to rearrange her life because of me, it meant the world that she did. My grandmother chose me and for that I would forever be indebted to her.

CHAPTER ELEVEN

It was the summer of 1989 - I was chilling at my mother's crib, looking at TV while I was supposed to be watching my sister. 'Queena was outside playing so I guess I wasn't doing a good job at watching her. That girl had a way of getting on my nerves, so if playing outside would get her out of my hair, then I was more than happy to let her have her way. She seemed to never do any wrong, but somehow always managed to get me in trouble – not to mention I always felt that she was my mother's favorite.

Anyways, she ran into the house screaming my name, "Monique, Monique!" I jumped up thinking something was wrong and she said to me, "Come outside."

"No, I don't feel like it," I groaned.

"Come on, come outside please!"

"I said no!" I exclaimed as I continued watching my show. Only moments passed before she came back in begging me to come out - apparently there was a boy that she wanted me to meet. I didn't care, I didn't want to go outside, but I eventually decided to go out since she was getting on my nerves and I figured it would shut her up once and for all. I put on sneaks and went outside. When I saw him, I ran back inside to fix myself up. He was fine! Hair combed, earrings on, neat clothes – he was the *whole* package. I finished primping and uttered, *Let's try this again*, before making my official entrance.

I felt like Patti LaBelle; I went outside with a new attitude! I was introduced to Vernon by my sister, and he and I talked for hours and we talked about everything. We exchanged phone numbers and made plans to meet the next day. There was something about Vernon that I couldn't put my hands on; he wasn't just a cute face - the connection that he and I had was unbelievable. We developed somewhat of a relationship; since we were young and were only going to be around each other for a couple of weeks, we didn't have much time to explore beyond that. I lived in Delaware with my grandmother and was only at my mom's during the summer and he was only at his aunt's house watching his cousin.

Before school started and we went our separate ways, we made plans to try to meet every weekend and decided to call each other at least once a week because, back then, you had to pay to make a long-distance call. It was so hard not seeing Vernon every day. I was in love with that boy. He made me feel like no other guy had made me feel before and that was special. He genuinely cared about me and I knew it because I could feel it in the words that he spoke and how attentive he was to me. He wanted to be around me and didn't seem to have any ulterior motives.

Eventually, I got into trouble with my grandmother by being sassy and lying to her and she told me that I had to live with my mom. As much as I hated the idea of living with my mother again, I was happy that I would be closer to Vernon. Once I moved back to my mom's, I saw or talked to Vernon every single day and my whole world changed. He was always on my mind and I reserved a place just for him in my heart.

"I'm going to marry you one day," Vernon insisted as we sat on cinderblocks outside of mom's house the day I moved back. My face burned from the blushing and I was a bit speechless. Though I couldn't say it, I felt that what he was saying would one day come true. I was falling for him and I falling for him hard.

CHAPTER TWELVE

Babysitter became my middle name. I was often tasked with watching my Aunt Stacy's kids, and had done so for a while once I moved back in with mom. On one particular night, her husband, Allen, came home acting a little strange; he was pacing back and forth like he didn't know where he wanted to go or something. I didn't know what was wrong with him, and frankly I didn't care. He finally gathered himself and proceeded to question me.

"How long has Stacy been out?" he asked me after he finally gathered himself together. I shrugged because she had been out for a while and it wasn't like I was keeping tabs on her. "You know when she coming back?"

I shrugged again, but this time gave him an estimated answer so he'd leave me alone, and with that, he went upstairs.

After about 10 to 15 minutes, I figured I would call Vernon and start washing dishes since two of the kids fell asleep and Lewis Jr., my cousin, was watching TV. While I continued to tidy up and enjoy Vernon's company, Allen managed to creep downstairs. His presence startled me, but not because I didn't realize he was behind me, but because of what he was doing behind me. Out of nowhere, I felt his body up against mine as he started to grind on me. I jolted backwards, almost causing myself to lose balance.

"What are you doing?!" I exclaimed.

"Shhhh, Lewis is in there," he whispered as he motioned for me to be quiet. I could hear the TV still going and he wasn't making a sound, so he was bound to hear any commotion that was going on in the kitchen. "Come here I want to give you something," he insisted.

I shook my head. "No, I don't want it."

"What don't you want?" Vernon asked. For a moment I forgot I was still on the phone with him. Knowing he could at least hear me gave me a little peace of mind, but not for long because Allen continued to rub up against me, causing my long pink and white night gown to begin to hike up. I tried to ignore him but then he grabbed me from behind and my hands began to shake.

Vernon was talking, but I didn't hear anything he said; I couldn't take my mind or my attention away from Allen trying to have his way with me.

"Monique! Monique!" Vernon shouted through the phone. What's going on? What is it that you don't want?" he pried. I assured him it was nothing because I didn't want to believe that I was still in that God awful game. I just wanted out! Somehow or another I kept being dealt a crappy hand.

Now what did I do to entice him? As this question ran through my head, I began having an out of body experience. At that very moment, my body would not function the way I wanted it to. I couldn't get my words to come out of my mouth and I couldn't stop tears from streaming down my face. *Oh God*, I thought. *It's happening again!*

"What's going on?" Vernon questioned as I continued to whimper. I wanted to yell out but the words were stuck in my throat. When I didn't respond he said "I'm on my way!" and hung up. I heard him, but it didn't register at the time. Allen grabbed my hand as the phone dropped out of my other hand and pretty much dragged me up the stairs. Lewis sat right on the couch and watched everything but didn't budge.

Once in his room, Allen told me to take a few puffs of a joint and gave me a bottle of something bitter to guzzle. I was already numb to the thought of what was about to happen, so it didn't make much difference. He laid me on the bed and managed to compliment my butt just as he yanked down my panties and then his pants and underwear. He opened my legs and jabbed his penis into me. The pain was unbearable and it felt like his penis was in my stomach. The bed rocked back and forth and I lost myself; I spent too much time harping on these moments and allowing my fear to take over me and I was tired. When he was done, he climbed off of me and began mumbling to himself. I tried to jump up but couldn't; I was in so much pain, so I dropped to the floor and crawled towards the bathroom. I felt so sick and honestly I just wanted to die. Soon vomit spewed all over the place and the room would not stop spinning. I reached out to grab the tub for support and ended up falling flat, allowing myself to be vulnerable to the pain and the anguish that was inside of me, both physically and mentally.

Then the craziest thing happened. I thought of my aunt walking in the house and finding me like that - I was sure that she would somehow blame me, but out of nowhere I got a burst on energy and got myself together.

About five minutes later, I heard a knock at the back door and thought that it was my aunt – maybe she left her key and was trying to get in. I went to open the door and it was Vernon and his cousin.

"What are you doing here?!" I asked. I was surprised he was there, but I was so glad.

"What's wrong?" he asked, ready to barge in and fight.

"Nothing. Nothing's wrong boo!"

"Did someone do something? 'Cause you sounded like you were trying not to cry on the phone." I wanted to tell him what had happened so bad, but then noticed a steel pipe in his hand. Whatever he was planning on doing, he was going to do some damage and I definitely would have let him have at it, but I couldn't be sure what the outcome would be. I convinced Vernon that everything was okay and that he needed to go because my aunt would be home soon.

"Okay. I'll call you tomorrow." He kissed me and said goodnight. I waved at him with the most insincere smile and watched him leave, wishing I could just go with him. Despite what just happened, I knew that there was someone in the world other than my grandmother that loved me. A sixteen year-old walks clear across town that late at tonight to see about me is more than wonderful in my book. He loved me for real and there was no doubt about that.

After Vernon and his cousin left, I tipped toed upstairs, hoping not to run into Allen. Once I snuck by his room, I scurried in the room where I stayed and locked the door. I was awake when my aunt walked in the house but I didn't make myself known. I continued to hide out and sat in the corner of the room until I eventually fell asleep. I had stayed up so late, that it was late in the afternoon when I woke up.

I thought that maybe I just had a bad dream – maybe I just imagined it all and nothing was really wrong. Well that thought was short lived. As I stepped out of the bed the pain reminded me that it was no dream and that was just wishful thinking. I crept out of the room to go into the bathroom, and as I headed back, my cousin said something to me. I don't know what it was because I was too busy trying to sneak back into the room without being noticed.

"Stop being antisocial," I heard my aunt say. "Come down stairs." I was trying to figure out how I could avoid going, but I couldn't think of anything. I called my cousin Lewis in the room and asked if Allen was around.

"No he's not here," Lewis said. I almost instantly let out a deep sigh of relief and with that I trotted downstairs. I was trying to be normal but I wasn't talking and I guess it was obvious because I always talked. I decided to be honest and say what was wrong - I drank something last night that made me sick. I knew that wasn't the whole truth, but it was enough to buy me some "act weird" time.

My grandmother finally came to pick me up and she knew right away that something was wrong with me but didn't really read too much into it because Juanita told her that I was sick. The next day, we went to church and as I sat there in the service, I began to get really mad with God for allowing so many bad things to happen to me. The preacher was preaching about how loving God was and I was couldn't help but question how was that even possible. The way I saw it, someone who loves you would never let harm come to you. One thing was for sure - either God wasn't real or He just hated my guts.

Later that same day, we went back to second service and I began to freak out on the inside. I stared at the image of this so-called Jesus hanging on the cross, and all I could see was me being nailed to one too. I sacrificed my soul and my body to all these men and what was my reward? What was the benefit?

I was tired of being tormented and I needed to be free from carrying all my burdens. I jumped up, went to the bathroom, and began to cry out. *Why? Why was I chosen? Why won't this stop? Why must I bear this burden alone? Why do I have to try and pretend that everything was ok?* I must have been in the bathroom for a long time, because my grandmother popped her head into the bathroom to check on me.

"What's going on? Why are you crying?" she asked. I told her that I could see myself hanging on the cross, and I didn't want to be on the cross anymore. She looked at me with a puzzled look and as I stared into her eyes, I got it; I got the courage out of nowhere I blurted out what had been weighing heavy on me.

"Allen touched me."

We both immediately left mid-service to go to my aunt Juanita's house and the pastor tagged along. I was scared to go in the house but not because of Allen – I didn't want to upset my aunt, but I had no choice. I was exhausted from trying to be strong when I wasn't.

As I began to tell my aunt in front of Allen what he had done, he immediately began denying it and pretended to have no recollection of what I was saying. I sat there trying to plead my case, but it was a hard battle. It was my word against his – me against him. I knew it was going to be a tough war to win.

"Wait a minute," my aunt Stacey stopped me. "What color was it?"

I froze. I could not believe that she asked me such a bizarre question. Here I was, fifteen years old, pouring out my heart and seeking justice and *that's* what she asked me? I shut down. I didn't see the use in even trying.

Days went by and nothing changed; we still went to Aunt Juanita's house as if nothing happened. Angry, hurt, and somewhat confused, I just couldn't figure out why no one could see through his lies. I couldn't let that liar get away with what he did. I was going to call the police to have him arrested but then thought that they might not believe me either. I came up with ways to kill him but I could never actually follow through with any of it. Then I thought of ways to kill myself but knew that I wouldn't go through with that neither.

As time slowly passed, it became harder for me to understand how it was possible for things to seem so normal. I was still watching my cousins, still staying over her house against my desires, and she was still doing my hair. I was truly in despair. I didn't know if anyone could see my hurt, or if they could and chose to ignore it. I wanted to show how ugly I felt on the inside to everyone on the outside, so I took a razor and cut off my eyebrows. It took a while for anyone to notice my ugliness and when they did it didn't go as planned. I thought that someone, anyone would see my cry for help, but all they saw was a crazy acting little girl.

The very next day, as fate would have it, my dad called me to see how I was doing and I told him what had happened and the next thing I knew, my dad was at my aunt's house. He walked in and asked where Allen was. Once he got his answer, he went upstairs and started beating on him. My aunt ran upstairs and stopped my dad from hitting him, but the few minutes that my dad wrestled with Allen was the closet I had come to feeling vindicated.

CHAPTER THIRTEEN

At that point in my life, I sure could have used a friend and luckily for me Trina contacted me one random day. We lost touch for a while because she never stayed in one place, but somehow we always seemed to find each other.

As usual we would talk for hours, catching up with each other and filling each other in on things that happened - the good, the bad and the ugly - and no matter what it was, we shared it. It seemed like I always had bad news, but it felt good to finally have something good to tell her for a change and that was that I found someone special. I felt like Vernon loved me for me and not for what I had to offer. I told her how he was willing to fight to protect me and she said, "girl he's a keeper!" I should have known to be more careful with my words because she unknowingly brought my spirits down by asking what was he protecting me from.

Trina always believed me, so it was easy to tell her what Allen did, what my aunt had said, and how my mom mocked me, asking who was I going to accuse next and how I was "young, dumb, and full of cum".

I told her about how I tried killing myself but could never follow through with it. I turned to alcohol to numb the pain and started sneaking out the house to go to parties where I knew I could find some. One particular party I went to, I got so drunk I could hardly walk. I felt like I was going to vomit and I think everyone else did too, so they told me I had to leave and they put me out. A guy from the neighborhood came out after me.

"You're not going to make it home. You can stay with me," the guy said. With blurred vision and slurred speech, I drunkenly agreed. The next morning, I woke up in a strange bed, but the face was familiar. When I looked out the window, I could see the back of my aunt Juanita's house. I had to get out of there and get back home before anyone realized I was missing.

As we spoke, I couldn't help but wonder how was it that her mom was the one on crack but my life was crazier then hers? Before hanging up, Trina asked me to come to her sweet sixteen party in Philadelphia which was about a month away. She begged and pleaded with me, saying how it wouldn't be the same without me, so of course I did my best to get there. When I showed up at Trina's, she was already outside with a few of her other friends, but when she came to hug me it was if no one else was around. As she took me in the house to put my bags down and introduced me to her uncle, a weird feeling came over me, but I dismissed it and we went back outside.

We had the time of our lives, just being silly, having fun and enjoying one another's company. Her friends were cool too. We were having so much fun, that we didn't even realize we hadn't eaten. We all decided to get Chinese food since there wasn't many choices, so we walked to a nearby Chinese place and while trying to decide what to order, the guy behind the counter shouted, "10 minutes, we close, order now!" We all looked at each other and started laughing as we strolled out.

Hungry and without food, we went back to her place and ordered pizza. We had no supervision at all, so we were cutting up and acting the fool. We started playing a game where you had to pick a random name in the phone book and call them to see how long you could hold them on the phone before they hung up. It was stupid, but fun – especially since it was really late and some people were asleep.

Eventually, one by one, the girls fell asleep, but I was determined to be the last one because no one was going to put toothpaste in my hair or pull any other prank. Everyone was spread out everywhere on the floor, and when I was finally the last one standing, I went to sleep.

Soon, I felt a tapping on my back, but I didn't move because I had not been asleep long, so I thought that maybe I was imagining things since I was so tired. The tap became more forceful, so I opened my eyes, and when they finally adjusted, I realized it was Trina's uncle and he was hovering over me. I knew that it was too early for him to be waking me up to go home, so why exactly was he tapping me? He signaled with his right hand to come to him as he extended his left hand to help me up.

As I got up, I noticed him biting his bottom lip and it started becoming apparent why he got me up. He led me to the bathroom and ordered me to take my clothes off. I was determined that I wasn't going to let this happen to me again, so I rejected him.

"You want to get in the shower with your clothes on?" he asked.

"I don't need to take a shower," I replied.

"Take your d*mn clothes off little b*tch. Don't make me hurt you." I thought, *well just hurt me then because I'm not taking anything off,* but before I could say what I was thinking, he reached behind him and pulled out a gun. He pointed it right in my face and I knew I didn't have a choice, so I quickly took my clothes off and he turned on the shower.

"Get in."

I did. A few seconds later, he joined me and asked, "Why in the hell were you playing hard to get?" *Why didn't I just let him kill me?* I thought as he started to kiss my neck and rub against me. He had the biggest manhood that I ever felt and the thought of him trying to put that thing inside of me was even more terrifying than being shot.

After he got his jolly's off, I slowly stepped out of the shower to dry off, put my pajama's back on, and went back into the living room where all the other girls were sleeping. I sat up until everyone awakened. I tried my best to act normal, but it was obvious that something was different with me – after all I was just about the silliest one just hours before, so I turned to the lie that had always been there for me.

"I'm sick. I gotta go," I told Trina. I apologized to her and I asked to call my grandmother to come and get me. We still had hours before her party was over, but I couldn't sit around and be uncomfortable. I could barely look Trina in her eyes. She was happy and for once she was in a stable place in her life. I didn't want to be the one to ruin that for her.

The time came for me to leave and all I could do was cry. I had mixed emotions because I was leaving her party early after not seeing her for years, but I was also leaving her in the house of a rapist.

CHAPTER FOURTEEN

"Therefore now, O Lord, take, I beseech thee, my life from me; for it is better for me to die than to live."

— Jonah 4:3

I once heard someone ask, "Have you ever been sick and tired of being sick and tired?" With both hands raised, I declared that that was definitely me. At this point in my life, I was at my wits end and I just couldn't take anymore of anything. I decided that if God was really real, that He was going to have to prove Himself to me. I was tired of pretending, tired of smiling, and tired of carrying such a heavy load. So, I cried out to the Lord with everything that I had, asking Him to please be the God that my grandmother spoke of.

I gave God six months to help me. It was February and my birthday was in August so I wanted to be changed before I turned another year older. If He didn't show up for me by then, I was going to come up with a plan to take my life that could actually work, since in previous times I chickened out. As each week came and went without any result, I pleaded, "Lord help!", but I still wasn't convinced that God was hearing me. Taking my life was starting to seem like a good option.

I was in high school, and of course, trouble found me. There was this girl that kept messing with me every day because she thought I liked her ugly boyfriend. I kept telling her that I wasn't interested in him but she was so sure I was. I was still seeing Vernon – in fact, I was in love with him – so there was no need for me to entertain the company of anyone else. Actually, Vernon had become my best friend and I would tell him everything that I would have normally told Trina.

"I'm going to kill myself if things don't work out with God," I casually told him. A slightly awkward silence filled the air.

"I don't like that plan," he admitted. "Plus, if you did commit suicide, I would miss you too much." Even though I heard him, I wanted to do something for me and no one else for once, even if it was something selfish.

One month had gone by and still no answer from God, but I wasn't going to let that deter me from giving Him a chance to show up for me. I heard a song on the radio that encouraged me to hold on. The song said:

"Nobody told me that the road would be easy. I don't believe He brought me this far to leave me."

Then there was another song that the choir sang that said:

"He was there all the time. God was there all the time waiting patiently in line."

Those two songs made me think that perhaps God was there and that He was just waiting for me to sincerely cry out to Him with my whole heart. I had to cast my cares upon Him. Just when I started to feel that there was hope for me, the enemy knocked on my door, and I opened it.

I was watching a Lifetime movie, and a way to kill myself had become so clear; a way that would be easy and painless, so if God didn't show up for me, I was going to take a boatload of sleeping pills and end it once and for all. The very next day, the same girl that thought that I liked her boyfriend planned to fight me in the locker room after gym. I knew it was planned because when I went into the locker room to change, there were both boys and girls that were in there around my locker. There was no way that I was going to be punked – my nickname wasn't Miss Lady Tyson for nothing. We fought and of course I tore her behind up, but that fight landed me a five-day suspension.

My grandmother was going out of town for a convention in Savannah, GA., and since I was suspended, I had to go too. I didn't want to go to church the whole week because church was boring and for old people. Oddly enough, when I walked into the first service, I saw a whole lot of young people my age, and as service went on they shouted and gave God so much praise. I was intrigued by how happy they looked in praising God. I knew that they were not playing around and that their praise was sincere.

I went back to the hotel that night jealous of how happy they were. I wanted to experience that same joy - God knows that I could've used some joy in my life. I was tired of being burdened, so I cried out to the Lord with everything that I had, asking Him to please be the God that I heard about.

I sat in the next night's service still in awe of how they were on fire for the Lord. It was young people's night, which meant that the young people led the service. I was convinced that I wanted what they had. I started clapping my hands, mimicking what I saw them do and it was fun, but I didn't feel any different afterwards. I expressed to my grandmother that I wanted to be saved and she told me to get baptized.

On day three of the convention, something amazing happened. I was told to tarry, which means to call and wait on God at the altar. I called on Him and called on Him and called on Him.

"Call Him like your life depends on it," I heard someone tell me. I let those words marinate as I prepared myself to give my all to him. I shut my eyes tight and I called Him with everything that I had! JESUS, JESUS, JESUS, JESUS, JESUS! The more I called Him, the closer I felt to Him, and the better I felt. A couple of ladies got me up and walked me towards the back as they encouraged me to keep seeking God. They got me changed for baptism and all the while, I continued to call on God. When I stepped in the water, the Bishop said some words about me giving my life to God, and as I was being buried with Christ I'd rise with Him. I went down in Jesus name and when I came back up out of the water, I was speaking in tongues. I didn't know what happened but I knew I loved it. The feeling that I felt was amazing; it was like I lost 50 pounds and that I could float.

God came through for me with months to spare. I now had an understanding of what the song meant when they sang, "*I looked at my hands and they looked new, I looked at my feet and they did too!*" So many songs that I'd heard over the years became so crystal clear.

"*He's an on time God...*"

"*When I think of the goodness of Jesus...*"

"*Can't nobody do me like Jesus...*" and the list goes on and on. I had finally gotten God's attention and I was glad about it.

EPILOGUE

God made an obvious change in my life. My family, friends, teachers and even enemies saw a change in me. My grades improved, my attitude was better, my life had a whole new meaning! I graduated high school and college with honors. I married my best friend, Vernon, and together we have two beautiful daughters. I now love living and as the Clark Sisters sang, *"I like livin' this kinda life, I'm livin' a blessed life."*

I understand that God has a great purpose for me, some I know and some have not yet been unveiled. I understand that even now, my life is not perfect; I still have trouble, still go through storms, still hurt and I still cry from time to time. The difference is that now I have a God that provides for me, fights for me, and is always there to comfort me.

Why did I have to go through hell, you may ask? There was a time that I couldn't answer that question, but now I can tell you. God allowed me to go to hell and back because He knew that I would come out with the victory. Yes, there were times when I felt like I would never come out, but God took me through the wilderness so that I would be able to tell my story and encourage others that no matter what you went through or are going though, God can and will deliver you out of the hand of the enemy.

To the reader: I pray for you right now in the name of Jesus Christ, that you be made whole in every aspect of your life. That whatever or whoever may be holding you captive – that those bands be loosed. I pray that God touches your mind casting down imaginations and I pray that God mends your bleeding heart. I pray that from this day forward you will know that God is able to cleanse you. In Jesus name I pray. Amen!

If you haven't given your life to God, make a conscious decision to surrender your life unto Him. After all, He will do "exceeding abundantly above all that we ask or think, according to the power that worketh in you." -Ephesians 3:20

In my despair, God showed up when I truly surrendered my life unto Him.

THE END

Recreated by image left in my mind

A Special Note to the Reader

Though God delivered me from my oppression, there are times that I wish that I would have confided in someone. I feel that had I expressed my emotions, I wouldn't have had to carry such a heavy burden for so long. I admonish you to seek help if someone has violated you in any way.

Tell, Tell, Tell! Do not keep it a secret. For doing so only holds you in bondage to the offender. Don't be afraid to expose the pervert for they are not as strong as you think they are. The fact that they violated you proves that.

Don't believe the lies that they tell you to gain your trust or interest, like you are so beautiful, I love you so much, I won't hurt you, I'll give you whatever you want if you let me do, etc. – tell them *no thanks*!

Rape and molestation are wrong regardless of your age. Your body is your temple and should be treated as such.

About the Author

Monique Bailey (b. 1975) was born in Chester, PA. She is a child care provider and the author of her first book and autobiography, *In My Despair*. Monique has lived more than most of her life trying to cope with the traumatic situations that occurred in her life and has now dedicated her life to protecting her two daughters and pastoring with a mission to help others find their deliverance in God.

Made in the USA
Middletown, DE
14 July 2024